The Polish Portrait of Bon

Robert I. Frost

The Polish Portrait of Bonnie Prince Charlie

palgrave
macmillan

Robert I. Frost
Department of History
University of Aberdeen
Aberdeen, UK

ISBN 978-3-030-99938-4   ISBN 978-3-030-99936-0   (eBook)
https://doi.org/10.1007/978-3-030-99936-0

Cover pattern © Melisa Hasan

This Palgrave Pivot imprint is published by the registered company Springer Nature Switzerland AG.
The registered company address is: Gewerbestrasse 11, 6330 Cham, Switzerland

For Karin

ACKNOWLEDGEMENTS

Many people have helped me in the writing of this study. Olenka Pevny came with me to see the Polish portrait in the National Portrait Gallery (NPG) Store in Southwark; her trained art historian's eye spotted several features that an untutored historian had missed. Lucinda Lax of the Scottish National Portrait Gallery (SNPG) was generous with her assistance and accompanied me on a most enlightening tour of the Gallery's magnificent collection of Stuart and Jacobite portraits. Rab MacGibbon of the NPG was supportive above and beyond the call of duty and provided me with the technical data on the canvas discussed in Chap. 7. Mindaugas Šapoka supplied a crucial reference on the complex matter of the Sobieski inheritance, and Adam Mead provided much useful information on the Cullum family. Mike Rapport gave advice on Jacobite exiles in Revolutionary France, and Katarzyna Gmerek helped greatly with suggestions and leads to material in Poland. Jane Ingle of the Suffolk Record Office, Bury St Edmunds, was unfailingly helpful, as were Betty Milburn from the Spanton-Jarman Project, Alex McWhirter of the Moyse's Hall Museum, Bury St Edmunds, Dr Bernd Pappe of the Tansey Miniatures Foundation, Celle, Jo Langston of Christies, London, Dorothee Feldman of the Kunstsammlungen Graf von Schönborn, and Alexandra Moritsch, Marianne Hussl-Hörmann, and Camilla Tinnacher, all of the Dorotheum in Vienna. Several people read and commented on various versions of the typescript, including Peter Davidson, John Gash, Katarzyna Gmerek, Neil Guthrie, Michael Hochedlinger, Bruce Lenman, Stasia Link-Lenczowska, John Morrison, Murray Pittock, Dan Szechi, and the three anonymous readers for Palgrave. Their observations have done much to shape the final text. Finally, I am grateful to the audiences in Scotland, England, and Poland for the lectures I have given on this painting; their comments and responses have helped shape the research and the book. My greatest debts are to Edward Corp and Peter Piniński, who have been particularly generous with their time and their considerable expertise; they have provided much-appreciated encouragement and several important leads; above all, they have both forced me to consider my arguments very carefully. Where I have not followed their advice, I hope they will forgive me.

Finally, I would like to thank the National Portrait Gallery, the National Galleries of Scotland, the Suffolk Record Office, Bury St Edmunds, Moyse's Hall Museum, Bury St Edmunds, the Royal Collections Trust, the Piniński Foundation, the Minneapolis Institute of Arts, the Tansey Miniatures Foundation, the Dorotheum, and Philip Mould Historical Portraits for permission to use images from their collections. Materials from the Stuart Papers in the Royal Archives in Windsor are cited with the permission of Her Majesty Queen Elizabeth II.

Aberdeen, UK, September 2021   Robert I. Frost

CONTENTS

About the Author

Robert I. Frost holds the Burnett Fletcher Chair of History at the University of Aberdeen. He grew up in Edinburgh and studied Modern History at the University of St Andrews, where he developed an interest in Polish history. He studied for a diploma in Polish Language and Culture at the Jagiellonian University, Cracow, in 1980–1981 and wrote his doctorate at the School of Slavonic and East European Studies, University of London, under the supervision of Norman Davies, a revised version of which was published in 1993 as *After the Deluge. Poland-Lithuania and the Second Northern War, 1655–1660*. He taught at King's College London from 1987, and his second book, *The Northern Wars: War, State & Society in Northeastern Europe, 1558–1721*, was published in 2000. He moved to Aberdeen in 2004 and is writing a three-volume history of the Polish-Lithuanian Union for Oxford University Press. Volume One *The Making of the Polish-Lithuanian Union, 1385–1569* (2015) won the *Pro Historia Polonorum* Prize for the best foreign-language book on Polish history published between 2012 and 2017.

ABBREVIATIONS

AGAD   Archiwum Główne Akt Dawnych [Central Archive of Old
        Acts, Warsaw]
Anon.   Anonymous
AR   Archiwum Radziwiłłów. [The Archive of the Radziwiłłs]
attr.   attributed to
BL   British Library
Fig.   Figure
n.   note
no.   number
NPG   National Portrait Gallery
RA SP   Royal Archives, The Stuart Papers
SNPG   Scottish National Portrait Gallery
TNA   The National Archives, Kew
vol.   volume

LIST OF FIGURES

CHAPTER 1

Unknown Man

Abstract This chapter outlines the problem at the heart of the book. It describes a painting in the collection of the National Portrait Gallery (NPG) in London that it catalogues as "Unknown Man formerly known as Prince Charles Edward Stuart". Although experts on Stuart portraiture reject the identification of the sitter contained in two inscriptions on the portrait, the painting has never been researched in detail, despite having a provenance that is at least plausible and despite the fact that Clementina Sobieska, wife of James III Stuart, the Old Pretender, and mother of Bonnie Prince Charlie, as Charles Edward is popularly known, was Polish. The chapter briefly recounts the story of the Sobieski-Stuart marriage and relates how the portrait entered the NPG collection as part of a bequest from Gery Cullum, the last owner of Hardwick House, Bury St Edmunds.

Keywords Stuart portraits • Jacobite material culture • Stuart, House of • Bonnie Prince Charlie • Polish dress

Languishing in the National Portrait Gallery's store in Southwark is a painting of a youth in Polish dress (Fig. 1.1). It is no masterpiece, but it is a striking image and rather a fine depiction of its subject. He is shown wearing a sash round his waist over a lavish frogged coat known in Polish as a *bekiesza*, named after Kasper Bekiesz, a Hungarian associate of Stefan

© The Author(s), under exclusive license to Springer Nature
Switzerland AG 2022
R. I. Frost, *The Polish Portrait of Bonnie Prince Charlie*,
https://doi.org/10.1007/978-3-030-99936-0_1

Fig. 1.1 Unknown man, formerly known as Prince Charles Edward Stuart. (National Portrait Gallery NPG 1929)

Batory, King of Poland and Grand Duke of Lithuania, who was also prince of Transylvania (ruled 1576–1586). The *bekiesza* in the original is scarlet rather than the orange shade in the photograph displayed on the gallery's website. An ermine-lined cloak is held in place by a small gold chain. The subject stares out confidently from under his rakish soft cap, adorned with a feather. His right arm rests nonchalantly on his hip; his left fingers the pommel of a Polish-style sabre hanging from a leather strap over his right shoulder.[1]

Who is this confident youth? In the top left-hand corner a faded inscription—it is not clear whether it is English or French—declares him to be Prince Charles Edward Louis. At some point, someone clearly felt that this was not particularly helpful, so they added a gold-leaf gloss just above the sitter's left shoulder, which reads: PRINCE CHARLES EDWARD LOUIS/ GRANDSON OF KING JAMES the 2nd/ BORN at ROME 31st Decr 1720/Died at Florence 1788. If this claim is true, then the National Portrait Gallery possesses evidence that Bonnie Prince Charlie's known penchant for dressing up did not only extend to kilt and plaid, which he first donned to spectacular effect at a carnival ball in Rome in 1741, wore frequently to public events, and which, in 1745, "quickly and thoroughly...became part of his persona".[2] But are the inscriptions to be believed?

The identification is at least plausible. As is well known to Stuart historians—but is not widely remembered outside scholarly circles—Charles's mother was Polish, the ill-starred Clementina Sobieska (1702–1735), daughter of Jakub (James) Sobieski (1667–1737) and Hedwig Elisabeth of Neuburg (1673–1722). It was, however, Clementina's grandfather, King John III Sobieski (1629–1696), who drove the Ottomans from the walls of Vienna in 1683, whose reputation ensured that she was seen as an appropriate bride for James Francis Edward Stuart (1688–1766), known according to taste as James III and VIII or the Old Pretender. The unhappy tale of Clementina's short life is an established part of Jacobite romance. Imprisoned by her cousin, Emperor Charles VI, under pressure from his Hanoverian ally when news of her engagement leaked out, she was sprung from captivity by an Irish Jacobite, Charles Wogan, who was knighted for

---

[1] Heinz Archive, NPG 1929: **Called Prince Charles Edward Stuart**, by an unknown artist. Oil on canvas, 43 × 23³/₄ in. (1092 × 603 cm); own fair hair, brown eyes and eyebrows, youthful rounded face; Polish costume (or uniform) of black fur cap with aigrette, scarlet jacket with gold frogging, scarlet cape, open, lined with ermine; a green curtain, drawn back, reveals a column, right.

[2] Nicholson, Robin. 1998. The tartan portraits of Charles Edward Stuart. *British Journal for Eighteenth-Century Studies*, 21, 148; McLynn, Frank. 2020. *Bonnie Prince Charlie: Charles Edward Stuart*. London: Sharpe Books, 61–2. The suit was a gift from James Drummond, sixth Earl and third Duke of Perth: Wyld, Helen, Dalglish, John. 2017. "A slim sword in his hand in battle". Weapons fit for a Prince. In Forsyth, David, ed. *Bonnie Prince Charlie and the Jacobites*. Edinburgh: National Museums Scotland, 81.

his efforts. She duly married James in true romantic fashion in a midnight ceremony in Montefiascone in September 1719.

James was no romantic hero, despite displaying considerable courage at the battle of Malplaquet in 1709. Thirteen years older than his bride, he lacked the easy charm of his uncle Charles II, or his firstborn son. He was principled, but dull, dutiful, and an inveterate worrier. Lively and vivacious as a child, Clementina fulfilled her dynastic duty by giving birth to Charles on 31 December 1720, but, so the story goes, was gripped by post-natal depression after the birth of her second son, Henry Benedict, Duke of York (1725–1807). Devoutly Catholic, she fell out with James over the appointment of the Protestant James Murray (c. 1690–1770), titular earl of Dunbar, as Charles's tutor. In November 1725, Clementina demanded that the king's unpopular favourites, his newly appointed secretary of state John Hay, titular earl of Inverness (1691–1740), and his wife Marjorie († c. 1765), who was Dunbar's sister, be removed from court.

James refused in a spectacular public shouting match and then dismissed Dorothy Sheldon, a niece of James Dillon, Earl of Roscommon, who had been appointed as a nurse to Charles in 1722. Dillon was a leader among the French-based Jacobites strongly opposed to Dunbar and the Invernesses. Sheldon, a Catholic, had become close to Clementina, but was sent on her way after challenging Dunbar's authority. A couple of days later, Clementina fled from the court, taking refuge in the Ursuline convent in Trastevere, to the great glee of Hanoverian supporters. She agreed to return to the family in July 1727, but the reconciliation was public rather than private, and the royal couple increasingly led separate lives.[3] Clementina did see more of her children, but she developed a powerful religious melancholy, ate sparingly, devoted her life to charity, and died a troubled, reclusive figure in January 1735 at the age of 32. She was accorded a lavish funeral, attended by 32 cardinals, which only intensified Hanoverian glee. A magnificent monument by Pietro Bracci, commissioned by Pope Benedict XIV, was erected in St Peters in 1742 to a tragic victim of dynastic ambition.

Charles's Polish descent has not, however, persuaded scholars that the Polish portrait is genuine. It was acquired in 1922, one of eight paintings bequeathed by Gery Milner-Gibson-Cullum (1857–1921) of Hardwick House, Bury St Edmunds. The most important was a miniature of Charles

---

[3] For the best account in English, see Corp, Edward. 2011. *The Stuarts in Italy 1719–1766. A Royal Court in Permanent Exile.* Cambridge: Cambridge University Press, 137–172.

I by David des Granges, which the Gallery was pleased to accept, but the minutes of the Board of Trustees reveal concerns about the Polish portrait:

> The Director [James Milner (1874–1927)] expressed his doubt about this painting being anything more than a fancy likeness of the Young Chevalier, an opinion which was shared by the Director of the Scottish National Galleries, but the Trustees considered that it should be accepted as being of national interest.[4]

The opinion *was* that of James Caw (1864–1950), Director of the Scottish National Portrait Gallery (SNPG), as expressed in his January 1922 reply to Milner's query:

> My dear Milner,
> Christmas & New Year (& a fairly large rearrangement here) have come & gone since you wrote about your Polish portrait of the Young Chevalier. They have prevented me writing but I have not forgotten your query & now, with a day or two breathing space before beginning to bring all the portrait gallery things together again, preliminary to recharging that Collection (now imminent) I'd better say that I can't see it a portrait of Prince Charlie at all. If it is it <u>must</u> be fancy.[5]

The charge was damning: A fancy portrait is a painting deriving entirely from the imagination; the designation suggests that the painting is inauthentic even if it does seek to portray whom it says it portrays. Caw's verdict has stuck. Sir Roy Strong's judgement, in 1968, a year after he became Director, was equally dismissive and grandly couched in the third person: "Dr Strong feels that this portrait cannot be of Prince Charles Edward Stuart and that it should be classed as Identity Doubtful".[6] Sir Roy gave no reason for his characteristically trenchant opinion, but it has been widely endorsed by experts on Stuart portraiture. In his definitive study of Charles's image, Nicholson includes the painting in his "List of Significant Misattributed or Misidentified Portraits", commenting that there is "no

---

[4] Extract from the Minutes of the 348th Meeting of the Trustees of the National Portrait Gallery, 2 February 1922: Heinz Archive, National Portrait Gallery: NPG 1924.

[5] Caw to Milner, 3 January 1922, Heinz Archive: NPG 1924. The letter is contained in the file on the des Granges miniature, not the file on the Polish portrait, which is NPG 1929.

[6] Heinz Archive: NPG 1929.

facial resemblance" and noting that the NPG had demoted it to the rank of "unknown subject".[7]

The internet has rescued the picture from the decent obscurity into which this scholarly consensus had plunged it. It can be viewed on the NPG website, where it is listed under images of Charles, and it pops up on internet searches under his name.[8] Its renewed visibility suggests that it is time to revive the issue of its identification. For while the internet may well preserve the image for ever, the original gently moulders away unseen in the NPG store. A 1995 conservation report found problems with cleavage around the sitter's neck; the next report in 2000 detected deterioration, concluding that:

> due to the uncertain identity of the sitter, and the fact that the painting is not required for display, the best course of action will be to monitor [it], checking its condition every five years and avoid treating [it] until absolutely essential—probably when the paint begins to actually flake.[9]

There are no further reports, which suggest that the painting has not been inspected since 2000: the NPG has many claims on its limited resources, and it cannot devote time and money to a painting whose identity is more than doubtful according to the acknowledged experts in the field.

This book explores the mystery of this portrait. It has never been properly investigated, and the possibility that it is genuine has been too readily dismissed, not least because scholars have not considered its Polish dimension. Caw damned it on the most cursory of inspections: he was clearly far more interested in the holiday festivities and his SNPG rehang when Milner consulted him, while Milner did not present to his Trustees the opinions of all the experts he approached. Nevertheless, while in the possession of the Cullums of Hardwick, it was believed to be genuine and was twice put on public display: at the 1889 Stuart Exhibition in London, and

---

[7] Nicholson, Robin. 2002. *Bonnie Prince Charlie and the Making of a Myth. A Study in Portraiture 1720–1892.* Cranbury, NJ, & London: Associated University Presses, 138.

[8] http://www.npg.org.uk/collections/search/portrait/mw01245/Unknown-man-formerly-known-as-Prince-Charles-Edward-Stuart

[9] Heinz Archive: NPG 1929.

at an exhibition of Stuart and Cromwellian artefacts in May 1911 organ-
ised by the Cambridge Antiquarian Society.[10]
For some scholars have been prepared to accept the identification. Gery
Cullum, who bequeathed it to the NPG, did so because he believed it was
genuine and worthy of inclusion among the paintings of national impor-
tance he left to the gallery; less significant works were bequeathed to the
Corporation of Bury St Edmunds or Cullum's niece, Mrs Maud Gurney
(† 1954).[11] Cullum was no gullible amateur, but an antiquarian of some
distinction. He published widely on archaeology and genealogy, contrib-
uted articles to the *Dictionary of National Biography*, and closely studied
Hardwick's impressive collection of paintings and historical artefacts. His
scholarly work on the genealogy of the Cullum family was privately published after his death.[12]

Another scholar impressed by the portrait was Walter Biggar Blaikie
(1847–1928), a noted Jacobite expert, who published several source editions and studies of the 1745 rising, including Charles's itinerary, for the
Scottish History Society and bequeathed his substantial collection of
Jacobite material to the National Library of Scotland.[13] Blaikie was consulted by Milner in late 1921, and while he admitted to his disappointment "that I never got the pedigree of that portrait", he added: "Of its

---

[10] *Exhibition of the Royal House of Stuart. The New Gallery, Regent Street.* 1889. London &
Bungay: Richard Clay & Sons Limited, no. 180, 58. *Exhibition of Stuart and Cromwellian
Relics and Articles of Interest Connected with the Stuart Period at the Guildhall Cambridge,
May 15–20, 1911.* 1911. Cambridge: John Clay & Sons at the University Press, 10.

[11] Copy of the Will of George Gery Milner-Gibson-Cullum Esq. Dated 19th September
1921. Suffolk Record Office, Bury St Edmunds, E2/26/1. The paintings bequeathed to the
Corporation of Bury St Edmunds are exhibited online in the Spanton-Jarman Project, on the
website of the Bury St Edmunds Past and Present Society, which houses photographs of the
collection taken by a local photographic firm before its dispersal: https://www.burypastand-
present.org.uk/gallery-viewer/. The collection includes photographs of Hardwick House
before its demolition, and of many of the paintings that hung on its walls.

[12] Milner-Gibson-Cullum, G. Gery, ed. 1928. *Genealogical Notes relating to the Family of
Cullum from the Records of the Heralds' College, the Hardwick House Collections, Wills,
Registers* etc. London: Michael Hughes & Clarke. Much of the genealogical work was under-
taken by the journalist and distinguished writer on heraldry and genealogy, Oswald Barron
(1868–1939): see correspondence in: Genealogical papers of the Cullum family and other
papers: Suffolk Record Office, Bury St Edmunds, E2/37.2.

[13] Blaikie, Walter Biggar. 1897. *The Itinerary of Prince Charles Edward from his landing in
Scotland July 1745 to his departure in September 1746.* Publications of the Scottish History
Society vol. 23. Edinburgh: Edinburgh University Press.

authenticity I have little doubt".[14] Milner did not see fit to present Blaikie's opinion to his Trustees, however, despite Blaikie having considerably more expertise on the Jacobite period than Caw, who had published studies of Allan Ramsay and Henry Raeburn, and a book on Scottish portraiture, but was no specialist in Stuart or Jacobite paintings.

Helen Farquhar (1869–1953), a distinguished numismatist, is the only expert on Jacobite imagery who has taken the trouble to inspect the original, in a visit to the NPG in March 1922 with Lord Dillon. She knew Gery Cullum, and had seen the painting at Hardwick, but welcomed the opportunity to inspect it properly. She did have doubts, but devoted considerable attention to the painting and included a black-and-white reproduction in her definitive article on Jacobite portrait medals. She wrote that the painting, which she had seen in a good light, was "interesting, although not very resembling". She nevertheless concluded that "there can be no doubt it has always been intended to represent the Prince; but the likeness is less convincing than one could wish, and one is inclined to think the painter gave much play to his imagination and, perhaps, was not working from life".[15] The use of "perhaps" suggests she was rather less convinced by Milner's outright dismissal of the painting than she had been in a letter to him written shortly after her visit, in which she accepted his view:

> I heartily concur in your verdict that it was not done from life—it certainly is not like him,…it seems evident that like so many of Prince Charlie's portrait gifts to his followers a very slight likeness was all that was accomplished.…it is pleasing enough & I shall take advantage of your permission & illustrate it, I think, but with the caution which you advise.[16]

Farquhar was indeed cautious, but she felt that there was at least some likeness, albeit slight, and no longer concurred quite so heartily with Milner's view on the issue of whether the portrait was painted from life by the time she published her considered opinion. She accepted that it probably did depict Charles and was more open than Milner—who, like Caw,

---

[14] Blaikie to James Milner, Firbank, Colinton, Edinburgh, 21 December 1921. The letter is in the NPG file on the des Granges miniature of Charles I, not in the file on the Polish portrait: Heinz Archive: NPG 1924.

[15] Farquhar, Helen. 1923–1924. Some portrait medals struck between 1745 and 1752 for Prince Charles Edward. *British Numismatic Journal*, 17, 224–5.

[16] Helen Farquhar to James Milner, 1 April 1922. Heinz Archive: NPG 1929.

was no expert on the Jacobite period—to the notion that it might have been painted from life.

Farquhar's caution reflected the growing scholarly concern over Jacobite relics. As the Jacobite threat receded after the 1760s and, in particular, once James Macpherson, Robert Burns, and Sir Walter Scott began to weave their beguiling spell, Scotland and the world fell hard for the thrilling, tragic morality tale of the doomed Bonnie Prince, the classic flawed hero whose evident humanity merely added to his appeal. After Henry's death in 1807, the property of the exiled Stuarts was dispersed and from the 1820s, the market rapidly flooded with Jacobite material, much of it of dubious provenance.[17] There was no shortage of gullible sentimentalists willing to buy dingy strips of fraying tartan supposedly worn by the Prince, or fading locks of reddish hair allegedly snipped from his head by adoring women: the 1889 Stuart exhibition displayed no fewer than eight items claiming to contain the Prince's hair, and nine with his tartan. While the exiled Jacobite court spent considerable sums of money on portraits and carefully selected the engravers who spread copies round Europe, it lost control of Charles's image in the face of the inflated demand that followed the 1745 Rising (known as the '45).[18] By the mid-nineteenth century, there was no shortage of cheap and not-so-cheap images of the Prince in circulation, many of them fanciful or spurious.

Was the Polish portrait merely one of these images, mocked up by some unscrupulous dealer with an eye for a painting and a quick profit? This is the opinion of Guthrie, the most determined, knowledgeable, and effective debunker of spurious Jacobite relics, who uses the Polish portrait to encapsulate the problem:

> The so-called "Polish" portrait…is a nice illustration of the process by which an object with no apparent Jacobite significance was, either through fraud or credulity, invested with a fictitious Stuart identity and a reasonably plausible pedigree in the nineteenth century, and then, in a more critical age, questioned and eventually rejected. Sometimes this process has been too drastic …but [it] has in general brought a necessary relegation of the more

[17] See Nicholson 2002, 93–110.
[18] Corp, Edward. 2001. *The King over the Water. Portraits of the Stuarts in Exile after 1689.* Edinburgh: Scottish National Portrait Gallery, 98.

dubious pieces to the storeroom in yet another phase in the history of Jacobitism through its (ostensible) material manifestation.[19]

Thus, the default position of modern experts on Jacobite culture is a well-merited suspicion of every object that claims a Jacobite provenance, and the Polish portrait, condemned by guilt through association, has indeed been relegated to the storeroom. Yet, proper suspicion should not exclude proper investigation: Guthrie's "more critical age" has certainly questioned the identity and pedigree of the Polish portrait, but it has not examined it. As Guthrie recognises, however, sometimes scepticism has been too drastic. The Polish portrait did have a Jacobite provenance that was at least "reasonably plausible". What was it, and how plausible is it?

BIBLIOGRAPHY

HEINZ ARCHIVE, NATIONAL PORTRAIT GALLERY, LONDON

NPG 1924.
NPG 1929.

SECONDARY SOURCES

Farquhar, Helen. 1923–1924. Some portrait medals struck between 1745 and 1752 for Prince Charles Edward. *British Numismatic Journal* 17, 171–225.
Nicholson, Robin. 2002. *Bonnie Prince Charlie and the Making of a Myth. A Study in Portraiture 1720–1892*. Cranbury, NJ, & London: Associated University Presses.

[19] Guthrie, Neil. 2013. *The Material Culture of the Jacobites*. Cambridge: Cambridge University Press, 142.

CHAPTER 2

Provenance

Abstract This chapter focuses on Clementina Jacobina Sobieska Macdonald, a staunch Jacobite and collector of Stuart memorabilia, who donated the portrait to Hardwick House. She was said to be a goddaughter of James Stuart, and was the daughter of Allan MacDonald of Kinlochmoidart, who fought in the 1745 Rising, after which he fled to France. It tells the story of the Kinlochmoidart MacDonalds, their commitment to the Jacobite cause, and their fate after the defeat of the 1745 Rising. It considers the plausibility of the case that the portrait came into Clementina Jacobina's possession through her father.

Keywords MacDonalds of Kinlochmoidart • Polish portrait, provenance • Jacobite Risings • Charles Edward Stuart • Clementina Jacobina Sobieska Macdonald

Gery Cullum states in the entry that he clearly wrote for the 1889 Stuart exhibition catalogue:

> This picture was presented by Prince Charles to his father's god-daughter, Clementina Jacobina Sobieska Macdonald, who was related in blood to

© The Author(s), under exclusive license to Springer Nature Switzerland AG 2022
R. I. Frost, *The Polish Portrait of Bonnie Prince Charlie*,
https://doi.org/10.1007/978-3-030-99936-0_2

Flora Macdonald, and an ardent Jacobite....She bequeathed it to Lady Cullum.[1]

Guthrie dismisses this provenance, but there is no sign that he devoted any time to investigating it, perhaps because what he termed the "wonderfully-named" donor sounded too good to be true.[2] Farquhar was willing to accord the provenance more respect, considering it "direct", although she made no effort to study it.[3] Donald Nicholas, who published an impressive collection of portraits of Charles in an idiosyncratic attempt to decide whether he was bonnie or not, thought the Polish portrait was "gravely suspect", adding: "If it were not for the fact that the picture has an excellent pedigree, it is unlikely that it would be acknowledged as an authentic portrait of the Prince". Nicholas was easily persuaded by Jacobite pedigrees, accepting the so-called Gentleman in Red, a depiction of a young man in the uniform of the 2nd Dragoon Guards whose resemblance to Charles is scant, purely on the grounds that it was owned by the Jacobite Pole family. He did not pause to consider why the Prince would have himself depicted in a British army uniform.[4]

How "direct" is the Polish portrait's provenance? Clementina Jacobina Sobieska Macdonald was a real person with an impeccable Jacobite pedigree (see Fig. 2.1). Her father was Allan MacDonald of Kinlochmoidart, fifth son of Ranald MacDonald, 3rd of Kinlochmoidart, who died at Glenforslan in 1725 of a surfeit of sour cream.[5] Ranald was one of the original Jacobites. The Kinlochmoidart MacDonalds were a Catholic cadet branch of the MacDonalds of Clanranald, and Ranald fought in his clan regiment at Killiekrankie (1689) and Sherriffmuir (1715). His eldest son Donald, 4th of Kinlochmoidart († 1746), played a significant role in the 1745 Rising. Donald's clan superior Ranald, 17th chief of Clanranald (1692–1766), refused to join the rising, but together with Clanranald's son, Ranald MacDonald, Young Clanranald († 1766), Donald MacDonald

---

[1] *Exhibition of the Royal House of Stuart*, no. 180, 58. Cf. Cullum's note attached to the rear of the portrait, transcribed by Farquhar, and included in her 1922 letter to Milner: Heinz Archive: NPG 1929.

[2] Guthrie 2013, 142.

[3] Farquhar 1923–1924, 224–5.

[4] Nicholas, Donald. 1973. *The Portraits of Bonnie Prince Charlie*. Maidstone: Clout & Baker, 36, 46.

[5] Mackenzie, Alexander. 1881. *The Macdonalds of Clanranald*. Inverness: A. & W. Mackenzie, 99.

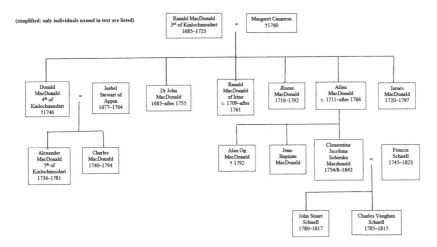

Fig. 2.1 The Kinlochmoidart MacDonalds. (Simplified: only individuals named in text are listed)

welcomed Charles on board the ship that had sailed into Loch nan Uamh on 25 July 1745 to launch the rising on a whim and a prayer. Initially doubtful about joining the cause, Donald MacDonald and Young Clanranald were persuaded—so the story goes—by the enthusiastic reaction of Donald's younger brother Ranald, who, when he saw them hesitate, told the Prince, "Though no other man in the Highlands should draw a sword, I am ready to die for you".[6] Donald MacDonald hosted Charles in Kinlochmoidart House from 11 to 17 August. According to his brother Æneas, Kinlochmoidart "was to have been made a baronet and peer of Scotland. He was an exceeding cool-headed man, fit for either Cabinet or field".[7] He raised a battalion for the Clanranald regiment, in which he was commissioned as colonel, serving as the Prince's ADC. He

---

[6] Browne, James. 1838. *A History of the Highlands and of the Highland Clans*, 4 vols. Edinburgh & London: Fullarton & Co, iii, 8; Macdonald, Rev. Charles. 1989 (reprint of 1889 edition). *Moidart; or Among the Clanranalds*. Edinburgh: James Thin, 167.

[7] Æneas MacDonald, "Account", *The Lyon in Mourning. A collection of speeches, letters, journals relative to the affairs of Prince Charles Edward Stuart*. 1895–1896, 3 vols. Ed. Paton, Henry. Edinburgh: Publications of the Scottish History Society, vols 20–22, i, 289–90.

fought at Prestonpans (21 September) and was wounded in October while directing siege works at Edinburgh Castle.

Sent north to persuade reluctant chiefs to join the rebellion, he was captured near Lesmahagow in November 1745, en route to rejoin the Prince at Carlisle.[8] Imprisoned in Edinburgh Castle, he was later taken to England, tried, condemned to death, and hung, drawn, and quartered in Carlisle on 18 October 1746; his head adorned the town's Scotch Gate for many years.[9] Donald's younger brother, Æneas MacDonald († 1792), was educated at the College of Navarre in Paris, where he became a banker. Charles lodged in his house immediately before the '45, and Æneas partly bankrolled the expedition. Against his better judgement, he accompanied the Prince to Scotland, holding a French commission, and has gone down in Jacobite history as one of the Seven Men of Moidart, the small body of companions who were the only followers the Prince brought with him, after the second ship in the expedition, carrying 700 French soldiers, was seized by the Royal Navy.

Much less is known of Allan MacDonald. According to testimony at his 1747 trial, Æneas was born around 1710; Allan was the next brother, so 1711 is the earliest he can have been born.[10] In late July 1745, after the Prince's landing, he accompanied Young Clanranald to Skye in an unsuccessful attempt to persuade Norman MacLeod of MacLeod and Sir Alexander MacDonald of Sleat to join the rebellion.[11] He was commissioned

[8] *A review of the two late rebellions, historical, political and moral. Part the first. Containing,* I. *A succinct account of the rebellion in the year 1715.* II. *The rebellion in 1745, to the end of the first consultation at Derby, as taken from the notes of General MacDonald, aid de camp to the Young Chevalier, 1745.* 1747. London: R. Baldwin junior, 46. Macdonald, Angus & Macdonald, Archibald. 1896–1904. *The Clan Donald,* 3 vols. Inverness: Northern Counties, iii, 301.

[9] Westminster Journal or New Weekly Miscellany, 1 November 1747, 257; Mounsey, George Gill. 1846. *Authentic Account of the Occupation of Carlisle in the 1745 by Prince Charles Edward Stuart.* London & Carlisle: Longman and Co. 264; James Steel.; *The Prisoners of the '45,* 3 vols. 1928. Ed. Gordon Seton, Bruce & Gordon Arnot, Jean. 3 vols. Edinburgh: Publications of the Scottish History Society, 3rd Series, vols 13–15, i, 146; Norie, William Drummond. 1903–1904. *The Life and Adventures of Prince Charles Edward Stuart,* 4 vols. London: Caxton, ii, 183–4, iv, 195–6.

[10] *The Trial of Æneas MacDonald, Banker to the Pretender at Paris.* 1748. London: Price, 14–15.

[11] *Journall and Memoirs of P...C... Expedition into Scotland &c. 1745–6. By a Highland Officer in his army.* In Lockhart, George. 1817. *The Lockhart Papers,* 2 vols. London: Anderson, ii, 481. The author of the account was almost certainly Alexander MacDonald of Dalelea.

as a captain in the Clanranald regiment, listed as serving from Kinlochmoidart with gun and sword with his second-oldest brother, Dr John MacDonald, a surgeon who had fought with his father at Sherriffmuir and who held a commission as a lieutenant in the Ecossais Royal. Unlike his elder brothers, Allan had no targe. Altogether, the Kinlochmoidart MacDonalds raised 80 men.[12] With the third oldest brother, Ranald, Allan was one of the ten captains of the Clanranald regiment who marched into England in December 1745; his younger brother James also joined the regiment.[13] They fought at Prestonpans (21 September 1745), Falkirk (17 January 1746), where the regiment played a key role in the battle, and in the sleet-lashed disaster at Culloden (16 April 1746), where it suffered heavy casualties.

There is some confusion in the literature over Allan's fortunes after Culloden. No fewer than five Allan MacDonalds served in the Clanranald regiment. McDonnell claims he was imprisoned, confusing him with another Allan MacDonald, a farmer from Borstill in South Uist, who served in the ranks.[14] Allan MacDonald of Kinlochmoidart evaded capture, however, and was probably among the "several gentlemen of the country" who gathered with Young Clanranald round Charles in Borrodale, near Kinlochmoidart, on 20 April, four days after the battle.[15] He is sometimes confused with the Reverend Allan MacDonald, a cousin of the Kinlochmoidart MacDonalds, who was the Prince's chaplain and confessor and held the honorary rank of captain in the Clanranald regiment. The Reverend Allan MacDonald accompanied the Prince in his immediate escape from Culloden and was among the "chieftans and 107 common men" who left Scotland with Charles in September. He landed

---

[12] Part of a Roll of Men upon Clanranald's Mainland Estates, with their arms; made up in the year 1745: *Historical and Genealogical Account of the Clan or Family of Macdonald from Somerlett, King of the Isles, Lord of Argyll and Kintyre, to the present period, more particularly as relating to the senior branch of that family, viz. the Clan Ranald.* 1819. Edinburgh: D. Stevenson & Co, Appendix, no. xxxvi, 37. *No Quarter Given. The Muster Roll of Prince Charles Edward Stuart's Army, 1745–46.* Ed. Livingstone, Alastair, Aikman, Christian & Stuart Hart, Betty. 2001. Glasgow: Neil Wilson, 146. The targe was the leather-covered shield carried by Highland warriors.

[13] *Historical and Genealogical Account*, ii, 166; *Prisoners of the '45*, i, 315.

[14] McDonnell, Frances. 1999. *Highland Jacobites 1745*. Baltimore MD: Clearfield, 46–7. *No Quarter Given*, 148; *Prisoners of the '45*, iii, 44.

[15] *No Quarter Given*, 146; Norie 1903–1904, iii, 193, 196.

in the Prince's retinue in Brittany and was later awarded a pension of 1000 livres by Louis XV.[16]

Allan MacDonald of Kinlochmoidart was also on board. He is named in a 1746 list of officers "newly arrived with his Royal Highness" in a regiment of two battalions led by Cameron of Lochiel († 1748), whose rank is given as brigadier; Allan is named as "*capitain dans le Regiment de Clanronnald*".[17] He was subsequently nominated for a commission in the regiment established in 1748 under the command of David Ogilvy (1725–1803), later the titular 6th Earl of Airlie, receiving a gratification of 1000 livres.[18] Allan's service appears to have been short-lived, however. The French military establishment was reduced after the treaty of Aix-la-Chapelle in 1748 ended the War of the Austrian Succession and brought peace between Britain and France. Under its terms, the French government withdrew its support for the Stuarts. It subsequently reduced its military establishment and expelled a recalcitrant Charles Edward from France. It seems that as a result, Allan MacDonald lost his commission and returned to Scotland. He is mentioned in a letter from his older brother John to Æneas in May 1751: "Allan and your friend Belly are still at Shunnaveg with your Mama and Ranny att Irine".[19]

Times were difficult, however. The scale of the retribution for the early and enthusiastic support for the '45 on the part of the Kinlochmoidart MacDonalds was by now clear. After the 1715 Jacobite Rising (the '15), rebel estates had been forfeited, but most had been recovered fairly quickly by their previous owners, often through the assistance of family members who had not supported the rebellion—sometimes with the aid of impeccably Whig friends, neighbours, and relatives bound by ties of obligation

---

[16] *No Quarter Given¸* 146–8; For the Reverend Allan MacDonald, see *Origins of the 'Forty-Five and Other Papers Relating to that Rising.* 1916. Ed. Blaikie, Walter Biggar. Edinburgh: Publications of the Scottish History Society. 2nd Series, vol. 2, 228.

[17] Liste des Officiers Ecossois qui sont arrivés nouvellement en France avec SAR. RA SP/MAIN/ 281/168.

[18] Etat des Gratiffications que le Roy a bien voulu accordés aux Gentilhommes Ecossois arrivés depuis peu en France. RA Stuart, 281/173; Second Etat des officiers Ecossois debarqués en Bretagne à la suite du Prince Edouard à qui Sa Majesté a bien voulu accorder des Gratiffications. RA SP/MAIN/, 281/177, printed in Browne 1838, iii, appendix xlviii, 469.

[19] John MacDonald to Æneas MacDonald, 22 May 1751: RA SP/MAIN/ 321/119. "Belly" is Isabel, née Stewart (1677–1764), Donald MacDonald's widow; "Ranny" is Ranald, the third brother. "Mama" is Margaret, († 1760) daughter of another leading Jacobite, Major Donald Cameron († 1718).

or patronage—and through the use of various legal subterfuges.[20] It was scarcely surprising, therefore, that the government decided to take a harder line in 1746, and the seizure of estates was carried out with much greater determination and efficiency.[21] Clanranald in general—and the MacDonalds of Kinlochmoidart in particular—had a reputation as a strongly Catholic and a particularly fierce clan. Murray of Broughton, Charles's secretary, observed that they were: "generaly speaking, the Acters and Abeteres of all the irregularities and outrages committed during the Rebellion" adding that the MacDonalds of "Moydart and Araseck [Arisaig] are hated and dispised by all their neighbours".[22] The lands of Donald MacDonald of Kinlochmoidart were therefore among the 53 forfeited estates that were to be administered by the five Barons of the Exchequer, who oversaw the operation.

Forfeiture did not necessarily mean eviction, and the networks of sympathetic relatives and connections still operated after the '45, although they were far less effective than after the '15. The Exchequer Barons inspected the claims flooding in from Highland gentry threatened with losing the property they had held from their clan superiors. After the 1747 Indemnity Act, which pardoned all but a number of named rebels, they were willing to allow families to continue to live on the estates pending a final judgement, but the terms were harsh: in 1750, Donald MacDonald's widow Isabel was granted an annuity of £500 Scots and possession of Kinlochmoidart House, which had been rebuilt in the French style just before the rebellion and burnt by government troops a month after Culloden. Margaret MacDonald, née Cameron, the aged widow of Ranald 3rd of Kinlochmoidart, was granted an annuity of £600 Scots in her own right; the heir was Alexander MacDonald (1736–1781), eldest son of Donald MacDonald. The concession was:

> To be Restricted during the Existence of the Heir male, procreat betwixt the Claimant and him, and during the life-time of Mrs. Margaret Cameron,

---

[20] Lenman, Bruce. 1984. *The Jacobite Risings in Britain 1689–1746*. London: Eyre Methuen, 168. For examples, see Sankey, Margaret & Szechi, Daniel. 2001. Elite culture and the decline of Scottish Jacobitism, 1716–1745. *Past & Present*. 173, 108–112.

[21] Sankey and Szechi 2001, 112.

[22] *Memorials of John Murray of Broughton, sometime secretary to Prince Charles Edward, 1740-1747*. 1898. Ed. Bell, Robert Fitzroy. Edinburgh: Publications of the Scottish History Society, vol. 27, 442.

mother of the said Donald McDonald, to a free Annuity of £400 Scots from Whit[sun] 1746.[23]

From 1749 until December 1752, the factor appointed by the Exchequer Barons for the Kinlochmoidart estate was Patrick Campbell, who treated the relatives of Donald MacDonald with particular severity. What this meant for the family is revealed in John MacDonald's 1751 letter to Æneas:

> Your Mama and friends here are making of a bad Mercat the best they can, and notwithstanding of their frequent losses and crosses from their old adversary are still, tho poor, hearty, and when they meet remember you & our friends there, in a Glass of Ferryntosh when better cannot be had, and wish that a large Salmon toute viff immediately out of the water, enough to regale twenty Frenchmen, could be magically conveyed to you wherever you are.[24]

Thus, the story relayed by the Rev. Charles MacDonald in 1889 that the aged Margaret MacDonald was carried dying out of the burning Kinlochmoidart House in May 1746 and expired in the garden 'before the burnt embers had cooled' is a myth: Despite the "losses and crosses", she was tough enough to survive until 1760.[25]

If the possibility of a return to normality after the Indemnity Act had tempted Allan to return from France, matters only got worse. The Kinlochmoidart lands were one of 13 forfeited estates annexed inalienably to the Crown in 1752, although the outstanding claims by "Subjects Superior" meant that part of the estate was still run by the Exchequer Barons until 1770 while they were investigated.[26] Although Ranald, the third son, received a tack at Irine in 1749 from MacDonald of Clanranald,

---

[23] *A Selection of Scottish Forfeited Estates Papers 1715–1745.* 1909. Ed. Miller, Alexander H. Edinburgh: Publications of the Scottish History Society, vol. 67, 314–5.

[24] RA SP/MAIN/, 321/119. The Ferintosh whisky distillery on the Black Isle was burned down in the 1689 Jacobite Rising—hence its attraction to Jacobites—but was rebuilt and became the first legal distillery in Scotland in 1690.

[25] Macdonald 1989. 186.

[26] The "Act annexing certain Forfeited Estates in Scotland to the Crown inalienably; and for making Satisfaction to the lawful Creditors thereupon; and applying the Rents and Profits thereof, for the better civilising and improving the Highlands of Scotland; and preventing Disorders there for the future", received the royal assent on 26 March 1752. The estates of MacDonald of Keppoch were also named, but were spared inalienable annexation: Smith,

and lived there for the rest of his life, there was no such grant to Allan, the fifth son. It was not until 1786 that Alexander's son John was to recover ownership of the estate.[27]

In such difficult circumstances for the family, at some point, Allan returned to France, probably after 1756, when hostilities between Great Britain and France resumed at the start of the Seven Years' War, raising Jacobite hopes of French backing for a Stuart restoration. It seems, however, that his expectations were not met, as is revealed in a letter, written after the end of the war, from an Alain Mac Donald seeking the advancement of his son, Jean-Baptiste MacDonald, "*issu d'une célèbre famille écossaise*" for a place in the royal stables:

> Monsigneur, le sieur Alain Mac Donald, former captain and chevalier de Saint-Louis, has the honour to inform you that he is a scion of the house of Mac Donald, known for all time for its attachment to the royal family of Stuart. He came to France in the suite of the Pretender with his six brothers. They had abandoned their property and their native land on account of the promises they had received that they would be recompensed in France for their sacrifices. Several of them were decapitated.[28]

The author can only have been Allan MacDonald of Kinlochmoidart; no other Allan MacDonald fits the profile. He rather exaggerated his family's exploits, probably to advance the cause of his son. Five brothers are

---

Annette. 1982. *Jacobite Estates*. Edinburgh: J. Donald, 23. *Scottish Forfeited Estates Papers*. 1909. Appendix, 350.

[27] Macdonald and Macdonald 1896–1904, iii, 299. Macdonald 1989. 186. Ranald died at Irine after 1761. Irine is now Roshven, Loch Ailort in Lochaber, on the coast at the foot of Rois-Bheinn, the highest mountain in the area. John MacDonald, 6th of Kinlochmoidart, was a major in the 21st Foot, the Royal Scots Fusiliers, which had fought on the government side at Culloden, and died of his wounds on 21 April 1794 during the storming of Guadeloupe.

[28] "Mgr, le sieur Alain Mac Donald, ancien capitaine et chevalier de Saint-Louis, a l'honneur de vous représenter qu'il est issu de la maison de Mac Donald connue de tout temps pour son attachement pour la famille roiale de Stuart. Il passa en France à la suite du Prétendant avec ses six frères. Ils avoient abandonné leurs biens et leur patrie, sur les promesses qu'on leur avoit faites de les récompenser en France de ces sacrifices. Plusieurs d'entre eux furent décapités". Printed in Clarke de Dromantin, Patrick. 2005. *Les Réfugiés Jacobites dans la France du XVIIIᵉ siècle. L'exode de toute une noblesse pour cause de religion*. Bordeaux: Presses universitaires de Bordeaux, 98. The letter is in the Bibliotèque Nationale, Nouveau d'Hozier, dossier 4906. Dromantin does not give the date of the letter, but it must have been written in or after 1762, when Ogilvy's regiment was disbanded.

known to have joined the '45 Rising: Donald, John, Æneas, Ranald, Allan, and James. The first three were arrested during or immediately after it. Of Allan's brothers, only Donald was executed, and he was not decapitated, but hung, drawn, and quartered. James was captured at Culloden, but escaped; John was captured in June 1746, imprisoned on Eigg, and then transferred to the prison hulks at Tilbury; he was released on 11 June 1747 for lack of evidence, and was lucky not to be executed, having been out in the '15. Allan seems to have escaped the attention of the government: unlike Æneas and his younger brother James, he was not named in the list of exceptions from the June 1747 Act of the King's Most Generous and Free Pardon.[29]

The letter states that Allan had to accept a rank lower than that of captain—*lieutenant d'haut bord*.[30] He is presumably referring to his return to French service after his time back in Scotland, as he is listed as captain in the muster lists from 1748. Allan states that he remained with his regiment until it was disbanded in 1762, when it was amalgamated with the Clare regiment. For all his disappointment, Allan seems to have remained in France, although there are few other traces of his life in exile. He was in Paris in January 1766, when he is mentioned in a letter from Æneas MacDonald to Andrew Lumisden (1720–1801), James Stuart's private secretary.[31] There is no record of his death. McDonnell suggests that he "fled to France and perished in the Revolution", confusing him with his son and grandson. The standard history of Clan Donald suggests that Allan married in France, where he had one daughter—Clementina Jacobina—and a son, Allan Og. Allan Og had a son and a daughter who, so it is claimed, married the Marquis Daringcour, given in other sources as d'Aveigncourt.[32] There was no such title in the French nobility, so this may refer to Jean de Falcoz, Marquis d'Arancourt (Harnoncourt), seigneur de Saint-André-de-Brioi s (c. 1743–1817), a deputy for the Second Estate at the Estates General in 1789. He died in Paris in 1817; his widow's name was given as Catherine Leroy de Sannerville, which suggests that if d'Arancourt did marry this unnamed MacDonald, she was his first

[29] *Prisoners of the '45*, i, 298.
[30] Clarke de Dromantin 2005, 98.
[31] Æneas MacDonald to Andrew Lumisden, Paris 20 January 1766: RA SP/MAIN/432/147.
[32] McDonnell 1999, 47; Macdonald and Macdonald 1896–1904, iii, 300. D'Aveigncourt is given by Mackenzie 1881, 98.

wife.[33] It is claimed that Allan Og and his unnamed son "were killed together" in 1792; the circumstances are unknown. Their cousin Charles MacDonald (1740–1794), second son of Donald MacDonald of Kinlochmoidart (see Fig. 2.1), enjoyed a more successful career in French service. He enlisted as a lieutenant in Ogilvy's regiment in 1757—probably alongside his uncle Allan—but later switched to the régiment du Foix, reaching the rank of major by 1778. He took part in several of the battles of the American War of Independence and was badly wounded at the battle of St Lucia. He fought at Savannah, and in 1780 proposed raising a Scottish regiment for French service.[34] By 1789 he was a colonel; he was guillotined on 24 Messidor, Year II (12 July 1794) on a charge of being a British spy, but no other MacDonalds are listed among those executed during the Terror.[35]

The revelation in his letter seeking patronage that Allan MacDonald had another son, Jean-Baptiste, whose advancement he was seeking, indicates how little is known of his family life in France. Clementina Jacobina's earliest years are as shrouded in mystery as the last years of her father. Who her mother was is unknown. Her birth date is widely given as 1768.[36] This would rule out the claim that she was James III's goddaughter, since he had died in January 1766. There is some confusion in the sources,

---

[33] *Archives Parlementaires de 1787 à 1860. Première Série: de 1789 à 1799, vi: 1789—États généraux. Cahiers des sénéchaussées et bailliages.* 1879. Ed. Mavidal M.J. & Laurent, E. Paris: Librairie administrative de Paul Dupont, tome vi, 545. Online version: Tome 6 : 1789 – États généraux. Cahiers des sénéchaussées et bailliages [Toul - Vitry-le-François]; http://www.geneanet.org/archives/releves/search_etat_civil.php?search=FALCOZ+DE+LA+BLACHE+D%27HARNONCOURT&id_table=5294&lang=fr, accessed 30 June 2016.

[34] Clarke de Dromantin 2005, 213–4, based on MacDonald's memoirs in Centre des Archives d'Outre-Mer, Aix-en-Provence, Colonie, E 295, dossier Macdonald.

[35] The two were "killed" together in the Revolution according to Mackenzie & Mackenzie, 1896–1904, iii, 300, and *Burke's Landed Gentry of Great Britain. The Kingdom in Scotland.* 2001. 19th edition, ed. Beauclerk Dewar, Peter. Chicago & London: Burke's Peerage and Gentry LLC, i, 866. Mackenzie states that Allan Og and his son "suffered together in the third year of the French Revolution": Mackenzie 1881, 98. For Charles's execution see http://les.guillotines.free.fr/guillo-m.htm, accessed 6 July 2016, and *List Général et très-exacte des noms, âges, qualités et demeures de tous les Conspirateurs condamné à mort par le Tribunal Révolutionnaire...1794.* Paris: chez le citoyen Marchand, le citoyen Berthé., le citoyen Channaud. Wallon, H., xi, 4–5. *Histoire du Tribunal Révolutionnaire de Paris. Avec le Journal de ses Actes* 1880–1882. 6 vols. Paris: Librairie Hachette et Cⁱᵉ, v, 387.

[36] Following Mackenzie & Mackenzie, 1896–1904, iii, 300.

however: a note in the Heinz archive claims that she was the goddaughter of Charles, not his father, which would be possible if she was born in 1768.[37]

This date is almost certainly wrong, however: in the 1841 census, Clementina Jacobina is listed as living on Kew Green, aged 86, which would mean that she was born around 1754 or 1755. She was a little younger if her tombstone in the graveyard of Kew Parish Church is to be believed; this claims that she was 82 at the time of her death on 12 November 1842, which would mean that she was born in 1759 or 1760; in either case she *could* have been James's goddaughter.[38] That she was born no later than 1758, however, is confirmed by her marriage bond and obligation, dated 7 June 1779, which lists her as "spinster, twenty one or upwards".[39] It would not be the first occasion on which an elderly lady was a little vague about her date of birth, which must therefore be dated to some point between 1754 and 1758. If she was born in 1754 or 1755, then it is possible that she was born in Scotland before her father returned to France to re-enter French service after the outbreak of the Seven Years' War in 1756, in which case her mother may have been Scottish.

It is unlikely that Clementina Jacobina was the godchild of either James or Charles, at least in the sense that the relationship would be understood today. Many did seek the honour, but not all received it.[40] Godparenting was, however, a well-established custom in eighteenth-century Gaelic culture, particularly among Catholics, and while it is certain that neither James nor Charles was present at Clementina Jacobina's baptism, it is probable that she was told the story by her father, and misunderstood the significance of what was more a symbolic relationship embodying notions of loyalty and protection. The sole source for the story is Gery Cullum, and the two different versions suggest some confusion and a

[37] Heinz Archive: NPG 1929.

[38] The National Archives (TNA), 1841 Census, accessed through ancestry.co.uk, 23 June 2016. The 1841 census does not list house numbers, but Clementina Jacobina resided at what was once called the Little Red House, number 77: A Link with Prince Charlie. Restoration of Old Monument, *The Times*, Tuesday 27 September 1938, 8. E. Beresford Chancellor claims that she was 88 at the time of her death, which accords roughly with the evidence of the 1841 census: Beresford Chancellor, E. 1894. *The History and Antiquities of Richmond, Kew, Petersham, Ham, &c.* Richmond: Hiscoke, 316.

[39] London and Surrey, Marriage Bonds and Obligations 1557–1921 for Francis Schnell, 7 June 1779, TNA accessed through ancestry.co.uk, 23 June 2016.

[40] Monod, Paul. 1989. *Jacobitism and the English People 1688–1788*. Cambridge: Cambridge University Press, 272.

misunderstanding of what the notion of godparent implied. He cannot have heard the tale directly from Clementina Jacobina, as he was born 15 years after her death, but he knew his step-grandmother, Anne Cullum, née Lloyd (1811–1875), second wife of Sir Thomas Gery Cullum, 8th Baronet Hardwick (1777–1855), who had been Clementina Jacobina's ward.

It was through Anne Cullum that the painting entered the Hardwick collection. She was one of two illegitimate children of John Flood of Flood Hall, County Kilkenny, the sister of W. Hanford Flood.[41] Her father was related to Henry Flood (1732–1791), the great Irish parliamentarian. Anne's grandfather had successfully challenged Henry's will, which, on the death of his wife, had left the bulk of his estate to Trinity College Dublin to establish a chair of Irish and purchase books and manuscripts for the College Library.[42] Perhaps on account of this difficult family background, Anne Lloyd was brought up by Clementina Jacobina.

How the women were connected is unknown. By the time of Anne Lloyd's birth, Clementina Jacobina had long been based in London. She enters the historical record on 7 June 1779, when Dr Francis Schnell (c. 1752–1823), a German scholar and mathematician, paid the Bishop of London £200 to issue the banns for their marriage in St George's, Hanover Square; he was listed as a Master of Languages.[43] According to Gery Cullum, Schnell tutored Ernest Augustus (1771–1851), fifth son of George III, from 1837 King of Hanover, although Cullum introduces some confusion by elsewhere claiming that he was tutor to Ernest Augustus's son George (1819–1878). The latter suggestion can be discounted. "Blind King George" of Hanover was born in Berlin and was brought up between Berlin and London; he was only four when Schnell died in 1823.[44] Ernest Augustus, together with his two younger brothers,

[41] Farrer, Edmund. Between 1921 & 1928. *Hardwick Manor House, Bury St Edmunds and its Evolution*. Place of publication unknown: Publisher unknown, 55.

[42] Kilkenny Archaeological Society, in Irish Archives Resource: http://www.iar.ie/Archive. shtml?IE%20KAS%20Q010. Accessed 23 June 2016.

[43] London and Surrey, England, Marriage Bonds and Allegations, 1597–1921, for Francis Schnell, 7 June 1779, TNA, accessed through ancestry.co.uk, 23 June 2016.

[44] In the note written for the 1889 Stuart exhibition, Gery Cullum stated that Schnell was tutor to Ernest Augustus: *Exhibition of the Royal House of Stuart*, no. 180, 58. In his note on the back of the portrait, however, he claimed Schnell was tutor to George: Heinz Archive: NPG 1929. Blind King George of Hanover was brought to Kew when he was four years old and had happy memories of the house on Kew Green later in life: Beresford Chancellor 1894, 323.

were sent out to lodge with a tutor "in a cottage" on Kew Green until they were 15. This cannot have been Schnell, however, as he is still listed in the tax records as living in New Ormond Street in 1783, when Ernest Augustus was already 14, and Clementina Jacobina's tombstone claims that she lived for 53 years in the parish, which means that she would have moved there in 1789, by which time Ernest Augustus had finished his schooling.[45] It is possible, however, that Schnell was engaged as a tutor before he moved to Kew. Quite what Schnell's ardent Jacobite wife thought in 1799 when Ernest Augustus was created Duke of Cumberland is not recorded.

Clementina Jacobina had by all accounts a strong personality and remained a fiercely loyal Jacobite all her life. She was described as "tall and commanding in presence", and died from her injuries after an "antiquated" headdress she wore caught fire as she stooped to kiss a child.[46] Why she should have left the portrait of Charles Edward to Anne Cullum, along with a scrap of tartan claimed to be a piece of the plaid the Prince exchanged for Flora MacDonald's dress, and a portrait of herself, is unknown.[47] It seems probable that the portrait may be that of an "unknown lady" displayed on the paintings from Hardwick on the Spanton-Jarman collection website (Fig. 2.2). In 1908, her portrait was described by the Reverend Edmund Farrer, who knew Hardwick well, as: "full face, curls on either side of the forehead, high muslin cap on head, and similar collar round throat. *Dress*: black with a lace fichu over either shoulder and meeting at the waist in front. Min. on it, 'Clementina Jacobina Sobieska Macdonald, wife of D[r] Schnell, cousin of Flora Macdonald god-daughter

[45] Fulford, Roger. 1973. *Royal Dukes. The Father and Uncles of Queen Victoria*. Revised edition, London: Harper Collins, 205, 281. London, Land Tax Records 1692–1932, Camden, St Andrews and St George the Martyr, 1782, 25; London Metropolitan Archives. Accessed through ancestry.co.uk, 30 September 2016. The princes lived in a house on the other side of Kew Green: Papendick, Maria Karolina. 2015. The Memoirs of Maria Karolina Papendick. In *Memoirs of the Court of George III*. Ed. Kassler, Michael. London: Routledge, i, 22. Papendick states that "the princes Ernest and Augustus were removed to the house at the top of the Green"; the princes William and Edward "were placed in the house, now the Duke of Cambridge's, with Monsieur de Bruyère": ibid. 30. For Clementina Jacobina's tombstone, see Piper, A. Cecil. 1943. Clementina Jacobina Sobieski. *Notes and Queries*, 185/7. 25 September 1943, 206.

[46] A Link with Prince Charlie, *The Times*, 27 September 1938, 8.

[47] Redstone, Lilian J. 1911. Hardwick House, Bury St Edmunds. *Proceedings of the Suffolk Institute of Archaeology*, xiv, part 2, 272.

Fig. 2.2   Portrait of an Unknown Lady. Other portraits from Hardwick House. Bury St Edmunds Past and Present. (© Spanton-Jarman Project. K505/3086)

of the Chevalier de St George [James III and VIII]'".[48] The role played by Clementina Jacobina's archaic headdress in her unfortunate death, seems to provide some corroboration. There is no other portrait in the Spanton-Jarman collection from Hardwick that remotely matches this description.

[48] Farrer, Rev. Edmund. 1908. *Portraits in Suffolk Houses.* London: Bernard Quartich, 161, no. 108.

Clementina Jacobina had two sons with Schnell, whose names betray her Jacobite sentiments: John Stuart Schnell (1780–1817) and Charles Vaughan Schnell (1785–1815). Both of them joined the army, served in India, and predeceased her by over two decades. She had three grandchildren, but a family dispute arose after her husband's death when Eliza, the wife of Charles Vaughan Schnell, decided to take her son, Francis (Frank) Macdonald Schnell (1811–1852) to India contrary to Francis Schnell's will, which stipulated that Frank must be educated in England or lose his legacy under the will.[49] It may be that this family dispute influenced Clementina's decision to gift her Stuart collection to Anne Lloyd, who married Sir Thomas Gery Cullum two years before the dispute came before the Chancery Court. Perhaps Clementina Jacobina's grandchildren, as servants of the Raj—John Macdonald Schnell (1805–1871), son of John Stuart, held a commission as a lieutenant in the Sixth Regiment of Foot—were insufficiently Jacobite in their sentiments.

The Hardwick collection was dispersed after Gery Cullum's death in 1921. He had inherited the house in 1875 from Anne Cullum, at which point he added the name Cullum to Milner-Gibson, his father's name. Her will, however, did not grant him outright possession, but created an entail of which he was the life tenant. Cullum never married, which caused a problem. Since Anne Cullum was illegitimate, and her nephews had also died without marrying, on his death the estate escheated to the Crown. He encouraged his niece, Maud Gurney, née Robertson, of Warwick Hall, Bury St Edmunds, to appeal to the Crown to recognise her claim to the estate, which she would have inherited had Anne Cullum been of legitimate birth, but to no effect. Hardwick's remaining contents were sold off and the house demolished. Some of the ten pictures left to Maud Gurney were auctioned after her death in June 1954 by her nephew, Brigadier Cecil Hay Gurney. Among the items sold were a portrait of Charles II, bought by the Duke of Grafton for £38, a half-length portrait of the Cardinal of York (£48), and what was claimed to be a Largillière of Charles, although Largillière never painted him (£27).[50]

Whatever Clementina Jacobina's motives for leaving her collection of Stuart artefacts to Anne Cullum, the claims that their provenance was

---

[49] *Reports of Cases decided in the High Court of Chancery by the Right Honourable Sir Lancelot Shadwell, Vice-Chancellor of England.* Volume VII, *Containing Cases in 1834, 1835 & 1836, with a Few in 1837.* 1937. Ed. Simons, Nicholas. London: J. & W.T. Clarke, 86–91.

[50] Anon 1954. Oil Paintings Auctioned. Sale of Bury Collection, *Bury Free Press*, 25 June 1954.

"direct" cannot be sustained. Flora MacDonald was a Clanranald, but was only distantly related to the Kinlochmoidarts, and it can be safely concluded that the scrap of tartan was not given by Flora to Clementina or her father, and is as clear an example of the sort of Jacobite tat that Guthrie condemns as could be found. Its provenance is a classic example about how pedigrees are inferred or implied by suggestion or assumption: the inscription on the back misdates the meeting of Charles and Flora by a year (Fig. 2.3).

The provenance of the Polish portrait is equally shaky. Gery Cullum's notes state that it was given to Clementina Jacobina by Charles, but that possibility can be dismissed. Charles was expelled from France in 1748, long before she was born, and although he made fleeting incognito visits over the next decade or so, during which his whereabouts are often unknown, it is inconceivable that he would have brought the portrait with him and donated it to a child. He could conceivably have given it to her

Fig. 2.3 Locket left by Clementina Jacobina Schnell to Anne Cullum. Moyse's Hall Museum Bury St Edmunds. Accession no. 1978.101. West Suffolk Heritage Services. The inscription on the back reads: Fragment of the coat which Prince Charles Edward Stuart exchanged for the clothes of Flora MacDonald June 28th 1745

father, but that possibility can also be dismissed, despite Allan's devoted service during the '45, and for all his attachment to the Jacobite cause, reflected in the names he gave his daughter. If Allan did become a Chevalier de St Louis, as the letter seeking his son's advancement claims, and if his granddaughter did marry a marquis, then he must have made something of a career for himself in French service, despite the hard-luck story he presented in his letter. It is unlikely to have owed anything to direct favour from the Stuarts, however. Since Charles refused to return to France officially, or cooperate with the French government after his humiliating arrest and deportation in late 1748, it is most unlikely that Allan MacDonald had any direct contact with the Prince or the Stuart court after 1746.

Charles may have waxed sentimental about his brave Highlanders in the empty years of drink-sodden frustration after the '45 that gradually leached much of what was bonnie from Prince Charlie, but he did precious little to reward them for their loyalty. As Marshal Étienne MacDonald remarked of his father, from South Uist, who, like Allan MacDonald, had fought in the '45 and fled to France with Charles in 1746, once he had secured a place in Ogilvy's regiment, "the Prince never gave him another thought".[51]

A 1755 letter from Alexander MacDonald, eldest son of Donald MacDonald (see Fig. 2.1), to his uncle Æneas, demonstrates that it was not the Stuarts, but a network of Jacobite—and, as after the '15, even non-Jacobite—sympathisers who looked after the children of families impoverished by forfeiture:

> Dear Cousin,
>   Tho I have not the honour of your acquaintance, yet being Cousins, I hope you will have the goodness to excuse the liberty I take in troubling you with this short line. My Father Kinlochmoidart left five sons whereof I am the eldest; the second is at Doway [Douai] with the Scotch Jesuites, but whether he designs to be one himself or not is more than I can determin; the third is with an English Esquire in the north of England, who takes a special care of him; and the other two are still with their friends in the highlands. Lady Lucy Stewart, my Lord Traquair's eldest sister,[52] took me upon my father's death, and gave me what education my family could afford, and afterwards between three and four years ago sent me to this College where I want for nothing, her Ladyship giving me Cloaths, pocket money, money

---

[51] *Recollections of Marshal Macdonald, Duke of Tarentum.* 1893. Ed. Rousset, Camille. New York: Richard Bentley & Sons, 125.
[52] Lady Lucy Stewart (1685–1768), sister of Charles Stewart, 5th Earl of Traquair (1697–1764).

to the paying fencing and dancing Masters, and it being thought proper and time, being now eighteen years of age, to launch into the world, my design is, God willing, to follow the military affair if I can get any incouragment in that way of doing, so if you thought proper, and would be so good as to speak or cause speak to the King to the having his Majesty's recommendation to some such persons he shall think fit to the procuring me some post in the army, I would be very much oblig'd to you and take it as a singular favour to the being a Cadet I do not choose if anything better could be done for me, we having many Countrymen and amongst others John MacDonald Cousin to Glenaladale, who has been these eight years Cadet without ever advancing. I shall not mention to you what our family has suffered upon the Prince's account, you knowing very well that my Father was executed, all lost and the Children reduced to misery...[53]

Æneas MacDonald was in no position to help either Allan or their nephew. He had already fallen out with the Prince in July 1745, as Charles suspected him of trying to persuade the Kinlochmoidart MacDonalds not to join him.[54] After a year in hiding following Culloden he surrendered to Lieutenant-General John Campbell on 13 May 1747, was imprisoned in Carlisle and then London, and testified to the Hanoverian commission following his trial later that year. His sentence of death for high treason was commuted because he held a French commission.[55] Charles regarded him as one of the many who, so the Prince thought, had betrayed him, unjustly suspecting Æneas of appropriating part of the Loch Arkaig Treasure, the money sent to Scotland by France that was buried during the rebellion. Back in exile in France, Æneas wrote regularly to James Edgar and then Andrew Lumisden, James's secretaries, stressing his straitened circumstances and seeking support, to little effect. Most of Edgar's replies were brief, but in one, written in November 1751, he stated that James "was pleased to express a particular concern for the merits and sufferings of your family", but added that "he is sorry that his own present bad circumstances do not allow him to give some relief & assistance to your Nephews". James had long given up all hope of recovering his throne, much to Charles's considerable annoyance; all he could offer was honeyed words and a characteristically deft passing of the buck to his son:

---

[53] Alexander MacDonald to Æneas MacDonald, Paris, 2 June 1755: RA SP/MAIN/, 356/27. For the role of Jacobite networks and sociability in sustaining those who suffered in the 1715 Rising, with similar examples, see Sankey and Szechi 2001, 114–24.
[54] McLynn 2020, 133.
[55] *The Trial of Æneas MacDonald*, 16; *Prisoners of the '45*, i, 68, 78.

HM on proper occasions is inclined to give them marks of his favor, out of the regard he has for them. HM took particular notice of what you mention about a Peerage &c for your eldest nephew, but he said that is a matter he cannot enter into, that it is to the Prince you must apply to on that subject, who knows better than he the services & sufferings of your family & who is no doubt very sensible of them.[56]

Thus, Æneas MacDonald was already thinking of the interests of his nephews three and a half years before Alexander wrote to him. He knew very well, however, that the Prince would not oblige him. It would be naïve to suppose that James's vague reference to "marks of favor" can be construed to mean that he had been showering portraits on the dispossessed Highland gentry, while there is no evidence that Charles was in any measure sensible enough of the "services & sufferings" of the Kinlochmoidart MacDonalds to offer them any tangible reward. Æneas did manage to secure a small pension from the French government—500 livres instead of the 700 sought—but his family continued to suffer.[57] As Allan MacDonald's letter on behalf of his son reveals, he was far from happy with the reward for the sacrifices he had made in the Prince's cause. Since his discharge in 1748, he wrote that:

> He had received from the Court none of the favours, which he believed he merited when he had moved from opulence to misfortune on account of his religion and the service he had given to a great prince.

It was for this reason that he sought advancement for his son, and he closed with a pointed observation on rewards that might be expected for doing one's duty.[58]

It was a complaint that could have been echoed by many former rebels. It was not portraits that the Kinlochmoidart MacDonalds needed. While Allan's older brother Ranald remained loyal to the cause, acting as an envoy from the Jacobite clans to the Prince in the summer of 1752 during the Elibank plot, like so many of the sons of the Culloden generation,

---

[56] James Edgar to Æneas MacDonald, Rome, 12 November 1751: RA SP/MAIN/ 327/50.

[57] Etat des Ecossois qui sont compris dans L'Etat de distribution envoyé au Superieur des Ecossois a Paris, November 1756: RA SP/MAIN/, 366/176a.

[58] "Depuis ce tems il n'a recҫu de la Cour aucune des grâces, que l'on croit mériter quand on est passé de l'opulence dans les malheurs pour la religion et le service d'un grand prince. Daignerez-vous, Mgr, le récompenser de placer au service, apprendront qu'on peut tout espérer quand on a fait son devoir". Printed by Clarke de Dromantin 2005, 98.

Donald's son Alexander turned to the Hanoverian state that had executed his father: he was commissioned into the Black Watch and fought in the American Revolution, dying in Edinburgh in 1781 from wounds received in the fighting.[59] His younger brother, Charles—the reluctant Douai student—was fighting on the other side. William King's famous criticism of Prince Charles—"I never heard him…discover any sorrow or compassion for the misfortunes of so many worthy men who had suffered in his cause".—may have been provoked by King's own disillusion, but it was well enough founded.[60]

Allan MacDonald, for all his loyal service, was too lowly a figure to have been gifted a portrait by Charles. While the Stuarts did distribute portrait medals widely among their followers, this was motivated more by the need to spread Jacobite propaganda than any desire to reward their supporters. The Stuarts did not give large oil paintings to captains in clan regiments: as important a figure as Andrew Lumisden, Secretary of State to James and then Charles expressed his disappointment after the latter's death when he only received a snuff box from Henry Benedict "as a small token of remembrance for faithful service".[61] It was small indeed.

However impeccable her Jacobite genealogy, it is therefore difficult to believe that Clementina Jacobina acquired the picture from James, Charles, or, indeed, her father. Her tartan locket suggests that she was simply another sentimental Jacobite who had enough money to trawl the lively nineteenth-century market in Stuart relics. It is most probable that she acquired the painting by purchase or gift. Did her pride in her father's part in the '45 sap her judgement and allow her to be conned by a cunning dealer with a handy paintbrush and an eye for a sucker? Did she simply invent the story that she was a Stuart godchild to convince sceptics that the painting was genuine, afraid that she had been duped? Or did Anne Cullum embellish, misremember, or misunderstand the stories she had been told by the woman who brought her up when she told them to Gery Cullum? Whatever the truth, it seems that the provenance, which persuaded some scholars to accept that the painting might be genuine, is indeed fanciful, and those who have doubted it were right to do so. No

[59] McLynn 2020, 408; Mackenzie & Mackenzie, 1896–1904, iii, 303.

[60] King, William. 1818. *Political and Literary Anecdotes of his Own Times.* London: John Murray, 201.

[61] Shield, Alice. 1908. *Henry Stuart, Cardinal of York.* London: Longmans, Green & Co, 104. Lumisden's snuffbox is now in the collections of the National Museum of Scotland, no. X.2015.105.2; it was included in the 2017 Jacobite exhibition: Forsyth, David, ed. 2017, 253, no.258.

direct evidence from Clementina Jacobina herself concerning the painting's provenance has survived. Wishful thinking and inferences drawn by others provide a classic example of the way in which dubious Jacobite provenances were created. Can the Polish portrait therefore simply dismissed as an odd curio that can be left in peace to moulder away in the NPG storeroom?

BIBLIOGRAPHY

Heinz Archive, National Portrait Gallery, London

NPG 1929.

Secondary Sources

Anon. 1954. Oil Paintings Auctioned. Sale of Bury Collection, *Bury Free Press*, 25 June 1954.

Beresford Chancellor, E. 1894. *The History and Antiquities of Richmond, Kew, Petersham, Ham, &c*. Richmond: Hiscoke.

Browne, James. 1838. *A History of the Highlands and of the Highland Clans*, four vols. Edinburgh & London: Fullarton & co.

Clarke de Dromantin, Patrick. 2005. *Les Réfugiés Jacobites dans la France du XVIIIᵉ siècle. L'exode de toute une noblesse pour cause de religion*. Bordeaux: Presses universitaires de Bordeaux.

Farquhar, Helen. 1923–1924. Some portrait medals struck between 1745 and 1752 for Prince Charles Edward. *British Numismatic Journal* 17, 171–225.

Guthrie, Neil. 2013. *The Material Culture of the Jacobites*. Cambridge: Cambridge University Press.

Macdonald, Angus & Macdonald, Archibald. 1896–1904. *The Clan Donald*, 3 vols. Inverness: Northern Counties.

Macdonald, Rev. Charles. 1989 (reprint of 1889 edition). *Moidart; or Among the Clanranalds*. Edinburgh: James Thin.

Mackenzie, Alexander. 1881. *The Macdonalds of Clanranald*. Inverness: A. & W. Mackenzie.

McDonnell, Frances. 1999. *Highland Jacobites 1745*. Baltimore MD: Clearfield.

McLynn, Frank. 2020. *Bonnie Prince Charlie: Charles Edward Stuart*. London: Sharpe Books.

Norie, William Drummond. 1903–1904. *The Life and Adventures of Prince Charles Edward Stuart* 4 vols. London: Caxton.

Sankey, Margaret & Szechi, Daniel. 2001. Elite culture and the decline of Scottish Jacobitism, 1716–1745. *Past & Present*, 173, 90–128.

CHAPTER 3

Resemblance

Abstract The main reason that experts in Stuart portraiture reject the identification is based on their contention that the face of the sitter does not look like Bonnie Prince Charlie. Yet, none of them have subjected the painting to close examination, and some experts on Jacobitism have stated that they do see a resemblance. This chapter compares the portrait to other depictions of Charles Edward and considers the problem of resemblance in the context of eighteenth-century ideas on portraiture and of the use of portraits by the Stuart court in Rome for purposes of propaganda.

Keywords Stuart portraiture • Charles Edward Stuart, appearance • Likeness in eighteenth-century portraiture • Charles Edward Stuart, portraits of

Perhaps the NPG is right, and its store is where the painting belongs, but the fact that its provenance does not stand up to scrutiny does not by itself disprove the contention that the painting is an authentic portrait of Charles, or that it was painted from life. For, regardless of the problem of its provenance, an important question needs to be addressed: if the portrait is not of Charles, then why would anyone have thought it was of Charles when the experts claim that it looks nothing like him? It is important, therefore, to address the problem of resemblance, for it is on the grounds of resemblance that the experts in Stuart portraiture have dismissed the possibility that the painting is authentic. In so doing, however, they raise important questions concerning the meaning of likeness and authenticity.

Not all the experts agree. For Gery Cullum was not the only person to believe that the portrait was authentic. In his letter to James Milner in December 1921, Walter Blaikie pointed out that the Marchesa Vitelleschi had used an engraving of the painting as the frontispiece to the first volume of her account of Charles and his daughter Charlotte, Duchess of Albany (1753–1789), adding: "I know that she thoroughly believed in it".[1] Blaikie is the only scholar even to attempt a proper comparison. He was suitably cautious, but concluded:

> The likeness to the Prince seems to me fairly good. It has a look of his mother & it is fairly like a portrait at Duns Castle said to be by Blanchet, at about the same age: it is not unlike the portrait bust by Le Moine—which I generally use as a criterion of resemblance.[2]

Blaikie's opinion suggests that it is worth taking a closer look at the issue, not least because not taking a close look ensured that when the pastel by Maurice Quentin de la Tour (1704–1788) of Henry, Duke of York re-emerged onto the market in 1994 everyone assumed, since the man who was shortly to become the Cardinal of York was wearing armour and posing heroically, that it must be Charles, an assumption that dated back to the early nineteenth century, before the portrait disappeared from public view in 1842. Then Bendor Grosvenor did look closely and established the sitter's true identity, which is now the settled opinion of experts in Stuart portraiture.[3] The facial resemblance to other portraits of Henry now seems obvious enough, although the image still appears widely on the

[1] Blaikie to Milner, Fir Bank, Colinton, 21 December 1921: Heinz Archive: NPG 1924; Vitelleschi, Amy, Marchesa. 1903. *A Court in Exile. Charles Edward Stuart and the Romance of the Countess d'Albanie* 2 vols. London: Hutchison & Co. The Marchesa, born the Hon. Amy Cochrane-Baillie († 1913), was the sister of Charles Cochrane-Baillie, second baronet Lamington (1860–1940). The good quality engraving she uses for the frontispiece was executed while the painting was at Hardwick.

[2] Blaikie to Milner, 21 December 1921. Heinz Archive: NPG 1924.

[3] Grosvenor, Bendor. 2008. The Restoration of King Henry IX. Identifying Henry Stuart, Cardinal York. *The British Art Journal* IX/1 (2008), 28–32.

web and elsewhere wrongly labelled, despite the best efforts of the SNPG, which now owns it.[4]

The misidentification suggests that certain cultural assumptions play a role in influencing impressions of "likeness". What is meant by "likeness"? Judgements on likeness are notoriously subjective, and nobody today is in a position to ascertain whether any of the portraits of Charles Edward painted from life really look like he looked at the time they were painted. What the experts mean, therefore, when they say of the Polish portrait "it does not look like" Charles, is that, in their informed—if subjective—opinion it does not look like other portraits of Charles. Opinion, however, is divided, and the views of Farquhar and Blaikie suggest that Nicholson's categorical judgement is premature, not least because some attested portraits of Charles do not always look very like other attested portraits of him, and because none of the experts who have said the portrait does not look like Charles have ever presented a detailed analysis to explain *why* they believe it does not look like him.

Such an analysis might begin by considering to what extent the sitter's features in the Polish portrait match contemporary descriptions of Charles. Two elements are in its favour: the sitter has brown eyes and red hair. While Horace Mann, writing in 1744, and Lady Anne Miller who saw the Prince in 1770, testified that he had blue eyes, most accounts, and the accounts of those who knew him best, agree that his eyes were brown or hazel.[5] There is no controversy over his hair: there are enough lockets containing it that are genuine to corroborate contemporary descriptions that it was chestnut, red, or reddish-blond. The eyes of the sitter in the Polish portrait are brown, and the hair is red. In these respects, the portrait matches contemporary descriptions. On the other side of the ledger, however, contemporary descriptions, backed up by many of the portraits of the Prince suggest that he had a long face, whereas the subject of the Polish portrait has a more rounded countenance.

[4] SNPG accession number PG 2954. https://www.nationalgalleries.org/art-and-artists/36356/prince-henry-benedict-clement-stuart-1725-1807-cardinal-york-younger-brother-prince-charles-edward

[5] Miller, Lady Anne. 1776. *Letters from Italy in the Years 1770 and 1771.* 2 vols. London: Edward & Charles Dilly, ii, 194. Nicholas suggested that "contemporary portraits and miniatures confirm that they were of that peculiar hazel which in some lights appears grey-blue, and in others golden-brown", which does not really help much. Nicholas 1973, 1. General opinion among experts agrees that they were brown: cf. Nicholson 2002, 37; McLynn 2020, 61.

Such evidence cannot be decisive either way, but there is enough to suggest that the portrait should not be rejected outright on the basis of contemporary descriptions. Moreover, in considering whether the portrait is "like", one first of all needs to bear in mind that, as Grosvenor observes:

> the Stuart iconography is full of instances where one artist has had to copy another's likeness, for neither James...nor his sons sat for their portraits as often as we might think...and the Stuarts instead favoured repetitions of what Prince Charles referred to as "the likest portraits".[6]

Thus, although the principal painters employed by the Stuarts in the 1720s and 1730s—Antonio David (1698–1737), Jean-Étienne Liotard (1702–1789), and Louis-Gabriel Blanchet (1705–1772)—certainly had full access to the princes when painting them, Charles's face in some portraits looks like his face in other portraits because they were influenced by, copied directly from, or were based upon, them.

Although Farquhar felt that the Polish portrait was "perhaps" not painted from life, she did not believe it was a fake, feeling sure that it was always "intended to be" a portrait of the Prince. To what extent, therefore, does the Polish portrait look like other, attested images of Charles? One might begin by considering Blaikie's observation that he detected a family resemblance to Charles's mother, Clementina Sobieska. It is, perhaps, best to compare the Polish portrait with an early portrait by Francesco Trevisani (1656–1740) in the SNPG. It was painted in 1719, the year of her marriage to James, and portrays her before she lost weight during and after her two-year estrangement from her husband between 1725 and 1727 (see Figs. 3.1a and 3.1b).

The Trevisani painting depicts Clementina at the age of 17, roughly the age of the subject of the Polish portrait. While her face is slightly thinner, it is possible to see the likeness that Blaikie discerned. Clementina has a high brow, the chin and mouth are similar, as are the set of the eyebrows, the brown eyes, and the prominent, gently curved nose. Clementina's eyes are slightly larger, but the set of the eyelids is similar.

With regard to portraits of Charles himself, it is best to begin with the image that Blaikie believed to show some resemblance to the Polish portrait:

---

[6] Grosvenor 2008, 32.

Fig. 3.1a Clementina
Sobieska by Francesco
Bertosi after Francesco
Trevisani (1719). SNPG
PG 886 (detail)

Fig. 3.1b The Polish
portrait (detail)

Blanchet's 1739 painting (Figs. 3.2a and 3.2b). It was commissioned by
Captain William Hay of Edington (1706–1760), an ardent Jacobite then
living in Rome, whose own portrait was painted by Domenico Dupra
(1689–1770) the same year.[7] It was Blanchet's second portrait of Charles;
the first, a magnificent image in full court dress, was painted in 1738 for
Dorothea of Neuburg, dowager Duchess of Parma (1670–1748), elder sister of Charles's maternal grandmother, Hedwig Elisabeth of Neuburg.[8]

---

[7] Corp 2001, 78. Hay's portrait is now in the SNPG.
[8] Corp 2011, 288; Corp 2001, 74–8; Nicholson 2002, 46–7.

Fig. 3.2a Prince
Charles Edward Stuart
by Louis-Gabriel
Blanchet, 1739 (detail)
Royal Collection,
Holyrood Palace
RCIN 401208

Fig. 3.2b The Polish
portrait (detail)

A cursory examination suggests that Blaikie was, perhaps, premature in claiming that it is "fairly like" the Polish portrait. The sitter's face in the latter is rounder, and his nose is not straight. There are similarities, however: the form and distance between the eyebrows, the high brow, and the shape of the chin and mouth, although the lips are a little fuller in the Blanchet (see Figs. 3.2a and 3.2b). All Charles's portraits show that his lower face was distinctive: observers commented on his "weak" chin and mouth—something that is most evident in the Lemoyne bust—pointing out that it was similar to his mother's, as indeed it was (see Figs. 3.1a and 3.1b).

While the Blanchet portrait displays a slightly thinner, longer face than the Polish portrait, there is one aspect of it that needs to be considered. Charles was 18 when Blanchet's portrait was painted, and 20 when it was completed in 1741.[9] It is unlikely, however, that it portrays him as he then looked. The Prince's face in the 1739 painting was largely based on a pastel by Liotard, dating from the summer of 1737, which James considered to be such a good likeness that he instructed Blanchet to copy the faces of his 1738 and 1739 portraits from Liotard's earlier painting (see Figs. 3.3a and 3.3b). As Corp observes, the Blanchet portrait is painted to make

Fig. 3.3a Prince Charles Edward Stuart by Louis-Gabriel Blanchet, 1738 (detail). NPG 5517

Fig. 3.3b Prince Charles Edward Stuart by Jean-Étienne Liotard, 1737 (detail). SNPG PG 1519

[9] Nicholson 2002, 47; Nicholas 1973, 16.

Charles look a little more mature, but the artist, aware of James's views, has not departed significantly from the model established by Liotard.[10]

Is this how the Prince looked in 1737? That summer he was 16 years old, while Henry Benedict was 12, yet Charles barely looks older than his brother in the companion portrait by Liotard. Indeed, as Nicholson observes, Charles scarcely looks older than in the 1734 portrait by David, when he was 13.[11] This image in its turn is a copy of David's famous portrait of the prince, seen as "very like" by James, which was painted in 1729, and therefore depicted him at the age of eight, although James asked David to paint him older than he actually was, so that the portrait could be used as the basis of copies for a few years to come (Fig. 3.4).[12] As it was.

The Polish portrait is clearly of a youth who is passing through or has passed through puberty, whereas the 1730s portraits by David, Liotard, and Blanchet depict the face of a child.

In this context, it is worth considering what "likeness" meant in the first half of the eighteenth century. What did contemporaries mean when

Fig. 3.4   Charles Edward Stuart by Antonio David, 1732 copy of 1729 original SNPG: PG 887

[10] Corp 2011, 285–8; Corp 2001, 74, 78.
[11] Nicholson 2002, 46.
[12] Corp 2011, 279.

they praised a portrait for being "like"? As Marcia Pointon observes, "likeness" as a concept "must be historically specific". She quotes Jonathan Richardson (1667–1745), who wrote in his influential 1722 work *An Essay on the Theory of Painting*:

'Tis not enough to make a Tame, insipid Resemblance of the Features, so that everybody shall know who the Picture was intended for, nor even to make the Picture what is often said to be prodigious Like. (This was often done by the lowest of Face-Painters, but then 'tis ever with the Air of a Fool, and an Unbred Person). A Portrait Painter must understand Mankind, and enter into their Characters, and express their Minds as well as their faces.[13]

Thus, when James praised the portraits of David, Liotard, and Blanchet for being "like", he did not necessarily mean that the images were "prodigious like" or a mere "resemblance" of their features. That was, as Richardson suggested, what even "the lowest of Face-Painters" could achieve. James did not employ fools or the Unbred, at least not by deliberate choice. He employed great artists, not mere Face-Painters.

James may have employed great artists, but he was fussy about the results of their work for a reason. Deprived of the throne that he believed was his birthright, he deliberately adopted an artistic strategy to proclaim to the world the legitimate status of the Stuarts as one of Europe's great royal dynasties, in a clear contrast to what he regarded as the Hanoverian usurpers, who, despite their descent from Elizabeth Stuart, daughter of James I and VI, had been mere dukes of Brunswick-Lüneburg, who were only raised to the status of electors of the Holy Roman Empire in 1692. James therefore commissioned magnificent portraits of his sons and of himself with all the attributes of kingship—the crown, the sceptre and the orb for himself; the orders of the Garter and the Thistle for his sons—to hang in the Palazzo del Re in Rome, and sent copies to those sympathetic to his cause: in 1716, James had overturned the stipulation of his father, who had revived the order of the Thistle in 1687, that the two orders could not be worn together, decreeing that the green ribbon of the Thistle should be worn round the neck.[14] This change allowed the two orders to be worn together, as a sign that the Stuarts rejected the 1707 Union,

---

[13] Jonathan Richardson, quoted by Pointon, Marcia. 1993. *Hanging the Head. Portraiture and Social Formation in Eighteenth-Century England*. New Haven & London: Yale University Press, 81.

[14] Corp 2001, 14–15, 16–17.

which had liquidated the separate kingdoms of Scotland and England to create the kingdom of Great Britain. It was a gesture that played better in Scotland than in England.

The Palazzo del Re, leased by the papacy as a home for the exiled Stuart court after it had to leave France in 1713–1714, acted as an unofficial British Embassy at this period, since the papacy recognised James as *de jure* king of Great Britain and Ireland, and many high-ranked British visitors passed through its halls during their Grand Tours or sought the help of the Stuart court in sorting out problems they faced in the papal states, where there was no official British representation. The Stuart court welcomed British visitors after the end of the War of the Spanish Succession in 1714. Protestants might be greeted by James's Anglican chaplain, for James by special papal dispensation, was permitted to provide for Anglican worship at the Palazzo del Re. James's officials could organise passports and introductions to Roman society, among many other services.[15] By no means were all of the visitors Jacobite sympathisers, but they came nonetheless: the exiled court elicited a strong fascination among the British elites in general, not least because James sought to outdo the Hanoverians in grandeur and display.

Portraits played a crucial part in that display, and numerous portraits were hung in the public as well as the private chambers of the Palazzo. James, in consequence, was not employing great artists to capture photographic likenesses of his sons so that they could be recognised in the antechamber. He was promoting an idealised image of a royal family with two healthy, handsome sons, in a deliberate contrast to the Hanoverian dynasty, which was wracked by conflict between the monarch and his heir throughout the 1720s and 1730s. George I and the future George II were barely on speaking terms before the king's death in 1727; thereafter, the son proved to be like the father, and the pattern was repeated. George II fell out spectacularly with his son, Frederick, Prince of Wales. By 1737, relations were poisonous, and in that year Frederick smuggled Augusta, his pregnant wife, out of Hampton Court palace when she was about to enter labour, to ensure that the king and queen could not be present at the birth. He was banished from court and established a rival court in Leicester House, which became a centre for opposition politicians down to 1751, when Frederick predeceased his father.

It was within this context that James commissioned the idealised, child-like images of his sons from David, Liotard, and Blanchet, which he regarded as singularly "like". For, while the facial representation of the princes certainly had to bear a good enough relationship to how they appeared in life, it is clear that James desired far more than what a mere Face-Painter could achieve: he wanted his sons to embody his idealised image of what young royal princes should be, and to project what James felt their character ought to be. Liotard was no fool: he was aware that James liked David's famous depiction of Charles, and his representation was clearly based upon it (Figs. 3.4 and 3.3b). James was delighted, and this is why he insisted that Liotard's portraits should remain the model for other depictions down to 1740.

Yet at precisely this moment, James began to lose control of Charles's image. In the summer of 1737, the 16-year-old Charles embarked on a tour of North Italy, during which he frequently escaped the close attention of his tutor, Dunbar, who accompanied him.[16] While in Venice, he had his portrait done in pastel by Rosalba Carriera (1673–1757), one of the most fashionable artists of the day (Fig. 3.5).

Fig. 3.5 Prince Charles Edward Stuart by Rosalba Carriera 1737. Piniński Foundation, Liechtenstein

[16]See Chap. 6.

Charles in the Carriera pastel looks older and more self-assured than in the Liotard and Blanchet portraits that James so admired. James was unimpressed and claimed that Liotard's image was a better likeness.[17] What did he mean, however, by "like"? There must be a suspicion that he disliked the portrait not because it failed to capture Charles's features, but because it did not embody his vision of what Charles should look like, because it did not fit his strategy of representation for his heir, and perhaps because Charles's firm gaze contains a hint of the defiance that he had exhibited on his northern tour. Carriera was far more than a mere Face-Painter; the portrait succeeds because she sought to express Charles's mind, and clearly, James did not like what he saw.

There are another two striking images of Charles, done from life in precisely this period, that were not commissioned by James, and which portray a much more mature individual than in the classic portraits by David, Liotard, and Blanchet. Giles Hussey (1710–1788) was an English Catholic from Dorset, who was resident in Rome between 1733 and 1737. He had good access to the Palazzo del Re, where one of his sisters was a servant of Winifred Maxwell, Lady Nithsdale (c. 1689–1749), the heroine of the 1715 rising who had sprung her husband from the Tower of London the night before his execution.[18] Hussey used his access to make drawings of the princes in his favourite medium of chalk and pencil between 1735 and 1737, showing Charles, unusually, in profile, with his hair tied back (Fig. 3.6).[19]

In Hussey's drawings, Charles looks considerably older than he does in the great paintings by Liotard and Blanchet; he is presented as the confident young adult who made his spectacular social debut on his north Italian tour. Seen in profile, which accentuates his high forehead, the Prince seems fuller of face, with a hint of the incipient double chin that was termed weak by contemporaries.

The Polish portrait portrays a young man who was already leaving childhood behind, at an age when the face undergoes rapid change before settling in its final form. The problem over what James considered to be "like", and the clear idealisation of his sons in the portraits painted by Liotard and Blanchet in the 1730s, suggests that it is worth reconsidering the Polish portrait in the context of the representations of Charles's face

[17] Corp 2001, 74; Corp 2011, 285.
[18] Corp 2011, 284.
[19] For another drawing, facing right, see Nicholson 2002, 55.

Fig. 3.6   Prince Charles
Edward Stuart by Giles
Hussey c. 1735/6.
Philip Mould
& Company

by Carriera and Hussey, rather than David, Liotard, and Blanchet, and that portraits of Charles as an adult might make a better comparison than the great paintings of the 1730s.

When depictions of his adult face are closely examined, the Polish portrait seems more "resembling" than has traditionally been allowed. Two elements of the Polish portrait apparently at variance with the images of Charles as a child—the roundness of the face and the shape of the nose—correspond more closely to portrayals of the Prince as an adult. To illustrate this contention, it is best to start with the 1747 bust by Jean-Baptiste Lemoyne (1704–1778) that Blaikie used as his criterion of resemblance. He did so with good reason. William King, who met Charles in London in 1750, stated that: "he has a handsome face and good eyes; I think his busts, which about this time were commonly sold in London, are more like him than any of his pictures that I have yet seen". King's servant also recognised the Prince from the busts on sale in Red-Lion Street "which were taken in plaster-of-Paris from his face".[20] Charles himself commented that the bust "was much admired for its being singularly like" (see Figs. 3.7a and 3.7b).[21] With a photograph of the bust taken at a roughly similar

[20] King 1818, 199–200.
[21] Quoted by Nicholson 2002, 82.

Fig. 3.7a Bust of
Charles Edward Stuart
by Jean-Baptiste
Lemoyne, c. 1747.
SNPG 594

Fig. 3.7b The Polish
portrait (detail)

angle, the case for the likeness that Blaikie saw seems good. The sitter in
the Polish portrait is marginally rounder in the face, but the bust's nose is
stronger than in the Blanchet portrait, and curves gently, as does the nose
in the Polish portrait. In both images, the hair is swept back and the forehead—which in contemporary descriptions is termed "high"—seems in
proportion, while the chin and mouth also correspond. With regard to the
shape of the face, it is known that the Prince's weight fluctuated, not least

from the testimony of Henry, who welcomed him back from Scotland in late September 1746 by remarking that his brother seemed fatter, much to Henry's surprise, considering Charles's long months of hardship in the Highlands.[22] Perhaps he took cream with his porridge.

There are portraits of Charles that portray him with a rounder, fuller face, such as the 1744 pastel by de la Tour, the original of which has vanished, but which is known from contemporary copies, the best of which is by John Daniel Kamm (born after 1702). The faces are portrayed at slightly different angles, and the de la Tour image shows Charles over a decade after the Polish portrait would have been painted if it is genuine, but once more, the brow is high and the nose is gently curved as in the Polish portrait. The set of the eyebrows and the distance between them are similar, as are the eyelids and the eyes (Figs. 3.8a and 3.8b).

Another portrait portraying a rounder face is by Cosmo Alexander (1724–1772), born in Edinburgh to a strongly Jacobite family from northeast Scotland, who fought in the '45 rising with his father, also a portrait painter, as volunteers in Pitsligo's Horse.[23] Forced into exile in late 1746, Cosmo Alexander lived in Rome between 1747 and 1751, where he painted Charles, though not from life, since the Prince refused to visit Rome after 1746, having fallen out spectacularly with his father. Nicholson stresses the influence of Dupra, and states that the first portrait,

Fig. 3.8a Prince Charles Edward Stuart. Miniature by John Daniel Kamm after Maurice Quentin de La Tour (1748) Private Collection Photo © Philip Mould Ltd, London / Bridgeman Images

[22] McLynn 2020, 254.
[23] *No Quarter Given*, 2001. 61.

Fig. 3.8b   The Polish
portrait (detail)

commissioned by James, was a free adaptation of Dupra's portrait of the Prince. He persuasively argues that Alexander must have seen de la Tour's portrait, by which it is influenced. Nevertheless, having fought in the Jacobite army, Alexander had certainly seen the Prince at first hand, and knew what he looked like. He served alongside his father, also a portrait painter, and it is not outwith the bounds of possibility that they sketched Charles during the '45. Alexander's last portrait is particularly admired by Nicholson, who praises "the liveliness and vitality to the facial features", drawing attention to the ghost of a smile on Charles's lips. Alexander's portrait again depicts the Prince with a fuller face (Figs. 3.9a and 3.9b).[24]

Alexander's image displays a good resemblance to the Polish portrait. Again, the eyebrows, eyes, nose, mouth, and chin display a considerable degree of similarity, while the shape of the face with the slightly weak chin—evident on the Lemoyne bust—is also apparent in both images. The face in the Alexander portrait is marginally longer, but shows a thickening of the neckline, as in the Giles Hussey drawings.

Two final comparisons might be made. The first is to the portrait identified by Grosvenor in the collection of the Earls of Wemyss at Gosford House and since acquired by the SNPG. It was painted by Allan Ramsay (1713–1784) in 1745 during Charles's stay in Edinburgh. It was long thought that Ramsay had failed to complete the picture, as his father's house was demolished shortly after his visit to Holyrood by a bombardment from the Hanoverian garrison in the Castle, but the portrait is now

[24] Nicholson 2002, 83–4.

Fig. 3.9a   Prince
Charles Edward Stuart
by Cosmo Alexander
(1752). Reproduced
from the Drambuie
Collection with kind
permission of William
Grant and Sons Limited

Fig. 3.9b   The Polish
portrait (detail)

accepted as genuine. It depicts Charles with a slightly narrower face than in the la Tour and Alexander portraits, but the principal elements of the painting again match the Polish portrait: the high brow, the eyebrows, with a good gap between them, the slightly curved nose, the mouth, and the chin (see Figs. 3.10a and 3.10b).

There is one feature of the Polish portrait that is not readily comparable to almost every portrait of the Prince: since the sitter is not wearing a wig, his ear is visible. There is, however, one adult portrayal of Charles in which

Fig. 3.10a Prince
Charles Edward Stuart
by Allan Ramsay, 1745
SNPG PG 3762 (detail)

Fig. 3.10b The Polish
portrait (detail)

the style of his wig leaves the lower half of his ear exposed: the pencil
sketch by Ozias Humphry, drawn from life in Florence in 1776 (Figs. 3.11a
and 3.11b). Charles's physical decline is evident, but the shape of the chin,
mouth, nose, and eyes, and the high forehead again are similar to the
Polish portrait. It is, however, the ear that is most interesting. Ears are as
unique to individuals as fingerprints and are now used extensively in foren-
sic identification, so it is worth having a close look. As in the Polish

Fig. 3.11a Prince
Charles Edward Stuart
by Humphry, 1776.
SNPG PG 2991 (detail)

Fig. 3.11b The Polish
portrait (detail)

portrait, the older Charles has a large ear with a somewhat elongated lob-
ule, a prominent targus, and a large, deep acoustic meatus. It is by no
means conclusive evidence, but it adds another element to the apparent
matches between the Polish portrait and images of Charles.

There is one more, iconographic element to take into consideration.
Nicholson observes that the Polish portrait contains no royal insignia.
Presumably, he means that Charles does not wear the orders of the Garter
and Thistle. Yet, it would not have been appropriate to wear them with

Polish dress—the Polish-Lithuanian nobility was fiercely egalitarian and opposed the creation of such orders. The sitter, however, is portrayed wearing a rich ermine cloak. While the wearing of ermine was by no means a royal monopoly, and many wealthy European aristocrats affected it in their portraits, nevertheless, ermine robes feature frequently in Stuart portraits, and in particular in portraits of Charles, alongside the orders of the Garter and the Thistle, as a convenient way of demonstrating his rank, since he could not be depicted with the attributes of kingship while his father lived.[25] Henry was less often depicted in ermine, but was acutely sensitive to the niceties of rank, like all his family, and was well aware of ermine's significance. As Sir Horace Mann reported, for his installation ceremony as a cardinal on 3 July 1747:

> [He] pretends to wear Ermine on his *Cappa* as a sign of Royalty, and consequently to take place of Cardinal Ruffo and all the other Cardinals, by whom he insists on being visited. All this and much more has alarmed their Eminences. Cardinal Ruffo went to Castel Gondolfo to expostulate with the Pope [Benedict XIV] upon it.[26]

His expostulations seem to have been successful: in his portraits as a cardinal, Henry rarely wore ermine.

The mere presence of an ermine cloak in the Polish portrait does not, of course, prove anything. Nevertheless, given the number of points of similarity between the Polish portrait and the other depictions of Charles Edward discussed here, Nicholson's dismissive judgement that "there is no facial resemblance" seems too categorical.[27] Those who, like Nicholson, have rejected the portrait as not "like" have for the most part never said *why* it is not like, and where they have, they have concentrated on one of several elements of the face: its roundness, while ignoring all the other elements that seem to correspond with known images of the prince, and have not considered critically the meaning of likeness in terms of eighteenth-century concepts of portrait painting. It would be premature to suggest

---

[25] In addition to the 1739 Blanchet painting (Fig. 3.2a), ermine robes feature in the following portraits: David (1726, 1729, 1734); Liotard (1737); Dupra (1740); Dupra (1742); Ramsay (1745); Strange (1745); Alexander (c. 1747, 1752); and Tocqué (1748), to name but a selection.

[26] Sir Horace Mann, 27 June 1747, quoted by Vaughan. Herbert M. 1906. *The Last of the Royal Stuarts. Henry Stuart, Cardinal Duke of York.* London: Methuen, 51.

[27] Nicholson 2002, 138.

that, in the absence of a convincing provenance, any of the points made in this chapter could establish that the Polish portrait is an authentic portrayal of Charles Edward Stuart painted from life—judging by the age of the sitter—at some point between 1735 and 1737. At the very least, however, the painting deserves further investigation to establish when, where, and by whom it might have been painted. First, however, it is necessary to consider the Polish context.

BIBLIOGRAPHY

HEINZ ARCHIVE, NATIONAL PORTRAIT GALLERY, LONDON

NPG 1924.

PRINTED PRIMARY SOURCES

King, William. 1818. *Political and Literary Anecdotes of his Own Times*. London: John Murray.

SECONDARY SOURCES

Corp, Edward. 2001. *The King over the Water. Portraits of the Stuarts in Exile after 1689*. Edinburgh: Scottish National Portrait Gallery.

Corp, Edward. 2011. *The Stuarts in Italy 1719–1766. A Royal Court in Permanent Exile*. Cambridge: Cambridge University Press.

Grosvenor, Bendor. 2008. The Restoration of King Henry IX. Identifying Henry Stuart, Cardinal York. *The British Art Journal* IX/1 (2008), 28–32.

McLynn, Frank. 2020. *Bonnie Prince Charlie: Charles Edward Stuart*. London: Sharpe Books.

Nicholas, Donald. 1973. *The Portraits of Bonnie Prince Charlie*. Maidstone: Clout & Baker.

Nicholson, Robin. 2002. *Bonnie Prince Charlie and the Making of a Myth. A Study in Portraiture 1720–1892*. Cranbury, NJ, & London: Associated University Presses.

No Quarter Given. The Muster Roll of Prince Charles Edward Stuart's Army, 1745–46. 2001. Ed. Livingstone, Alastair, Aikman, Christian & Stuart Hart, Betty. Glasgow: Neil Wilson.

CHAPTER 4

The Half-Polish Prince

Abstract This chapter discusses Bonnie Prince Charlie's Polish family, a topic that is largely ignored or downplayed in scholarship on Jacobitism. It considers the relations of James Stuart and his sons with Clementina Sobieska and her Polish family, in particular her father, Jakub Sobieski, and her sister, Maria Karolina, Duchess of Bouillon. It reassesses the character of James's queen, questioning the standard depiction of her as a monomaniacal religious fanatic, presenting her as a shrewd defender of her position, and of the interests of her sons. It looks at the question of the vast properties of the Sobieski family, and the complex question of the claims of James Stuart's sons to the Sobieski inheritance.

Keywords Sobieski family • Stuart-Sobieski relations • Clementina Sobieska • The Sobieski inheritance • Jakub Sobieski • James III and VIII

Helen Farquhar was the first to suggest a possible Polish context for the portrait, alluding to an alleged visit to Poland by Charles in 1749, and floating the notion that the picture was painted in connection with a possible candidature for the elective Polish throne.[1] The suggestion that the portrait might have been painted with a Polish audience in mind should

---

[1] Farquhar 1923–1924, 225.

© The Author(s), under exclusive license to Springer Nature Switzerland AG 2022
R. I. Frost, *The Polish Portrait of Bonnie Prince Charlie*,
https://doi.org/10.1007/978-3-030-99936-0_4

be taken more seriously than it has been. Apart from the dramatic story of Clementina's unhappy marriage and the occasional mention of her dowry, however, the question of Charles's Polish family connections has largely been ignored by writers on the Stuarts, with the exception of Piniński, who concentrates on Charles's adult life and his descendants. Clementina's relationship with her sons has never been properly explored in the anglophone literature, although Corp gives the question of Clementina's relationship with James a balanced and thoughtful assessment, and Aleksandra Skrzypietz undertakes a fundamental reappraisal in her forthcoming biography of Clementina, which is firmly based on a substantial body of new material from the Sobieski papers, which resurfaced in the 1990s in the National Archive of Belarus in Minsk, and which have recently been catalogued and made available to scholars.[2]

When standard texts on the Stuarts mention Clementina, most content themselves with a few remarks about her supposed religious mania, occasionally coloured in older works with musings based on national stereotypes: Shield observes—on what basis apart from prejudice is unclear—that "Clementina was naturally gay but of an hysterical temperament, as Polish women so often are".[3] Gaetano Platania, in similar vein, suggests that after the birth of Charles all that Clementina could do was "surrender to her religious instincts".[4] Clementina was undoubtedly pious, but religion was by no means the only matter in which she took an interest. Her defiance of James in the 1720s might better be portrayed as the courageous act of a woman willing to defy convention and take a stand against an act of male authority, the acceptance of which would compromise her religious principles. As Skrzypietz points out in her biography of Jakub Sobieski, Clementina's frequent letters to her father betray not a hint of psychological problems; instead, they show a determination, inherited from Jakub, to uphold the honour of her own royal house. As she wrote to her father from the convent of St Cecilia in February 1726: "I cannot forget that I am your daughter and the granddaughter of King John. If I had not reacted as I did [to James's actions], I would have betrayed my position and my birth, related as I am to so many European rulers".[5]

[2] Corp 2011, 137–172.
[3] Shield 1908, 3.
[4] Platania, Gaetano. 1980. Angielskie małżeństwo Marii Klementyny. *Sobótka*, 35/2, 408.
[5] Clementina to Jakub Sobieski, 2 February 1726, quoted by Skrzypietz, Aleksandra. 2015. *Jakub Sobieski*. Poznań: Wydawnictwo Poznańskie, 333. Through her mother, Clementina was a cousin of the emperor, Charles VI.

This is not the voice of the hysterical, tragic queen starving herself in self-imposed religious isolation that appears in so many accounts. Clementina was far more involved in worldly affairs than this image suggests. Brought up in Silesia, she did not speak or read Polish, but she was well aware of her Polish background, and her royal status.[6] It was the issue of her status, rather than the problem of Charles being put under Dunbar's care, that lay behind the clash with James in 1725. James's refusal to allow her to have her own court and control of her household, as was normal practice among ruling houses, had cast a shadow over the relationship from the outset: Dunbar's appointment was merely the last indignity inflicted upon James's spirited young queen.

Clementina was forced to accept the servants that James selected for her, an imposition that she began to challenge vociferously long before she absconded.[7] The problem came to a head during Clementina's second pregnancy, when James decided, without consulting her, that to save money, Charles would be removed from the care of women after the birth. Charles was only four when Henry was born; it was normal practice to wait until a male child was seven before this step was taken. When it became clear that he was to be entrusted to the care of James's favourite Dunbar, who was to be the young prince's tutor, relations broke down. Dunbar was hated by Clementina, who was now unable to see her son without him being present.[8]

Clementina's volcanic reaction to Dunbar's appointment was a calculated political move. As she was well aware, Dunbar and the Invernesses were deeply unpopular with wide circles at the Jacobite court, and her intransigence over the next two years was sustained by her knowledge of the extent of the support for their removal from court and by the backing of Pope Benedict XIII. Both these factors played their part in the queen's ultimate—if partial—victory, in which she returned to court and was granted her own household.

Clementina's anger at Dunbar's appointment may well have been inspired in part by a desire to ensure that Charles's prospects of securing the Polish throne were not fatally damaged. This prospect was, in many respects, a more viable option than the return of James or one of his sons to the British throne, which would have required military action to force

[6] Skrzypietz 2015, 312.
[7] Corp 2011, 131–4.
[8] Corp 2011, 156–7, 163.

a Catholic king on the Protestant political establishments in England and Scotland, both of which had rejected James II in 1688 and 1689 respectively. The throne of Poland-Lithuania was elective. Stuart princes, including James II himself, had often been mentioned as potential candidates, but James had rejected suggestions that he should become a candidate in 1697 on the death of John Sobieski, for fear it might compromise any return to the British throne.[9] Nevertheless, in due course, as an adult and a Catholic, Charles—or Henry—would have had far more realistic prospects of election to the Polish throne than either would have of forcing himself on the reluctant British.

Clementina grew up with as much resentment for the loss of the Polish throne by her father as her husband did with regard to the loss of the British throne by his. Nevertheless, she did not push Charles's cause in 1732, when Augustus II died. Charles was only 11, and he would not have stood a chance of election at that age; furthermore, she knew that her father, still smarting over his defeat by Augustus in 1697, was considering putting himself forward once more. Clementina was not in favour, perhaps because she felt it might damage the long-term prospects of her sons. She had close links to Stanisław Leszczyński (1677–1766), the French-backed candidate who had been chosen king in 1704 in a sham election insisted on by Charles XII of Sweden, and who sought the throne once again in 1733, and she urged her father not to be tempted.[10] Jakub took his daughter's advice and distanced himself from the bitter struggles around the election, which sparked the War of the Polish Succession (1733–1735) in which Augustus's son Augustus III (1696–1763) finally secured the throne with Russian backing.

Clementina's death buried the matter once and for all. Augustus was to reign until his death in 1763. Charles was well aware of his Polish roots and had several contacts with Poland in the years after the '45, and in late 1746, he was urging Henry and James to contract a marriage for the former with one of their fabulously wealthy Radziwiłł cousins, while from April 1748, he was conducting a passionate affair with his Polish cousin, Marie-Louise de la Trémouille, Princess of Talmont, who was 20 years his

---

[9] For James's candidature in the 1650s, see Frost, Robert. 1993. *After the Deluge. Poland-Lithuania and the Second Northern War 1655–1660*. Cambridge, Cambridge University Press, 165–6.

[10] Clementina to Jakub Sobieski, Rome, 28 March 1733, *Sobiesciana z archiwum hr. Przezdzieckich w Warszawie*. 1883. Ed. Leniek, Jan. Cracow: Czas, 26, no. 122.

senior. She was a granddaughter of Stanisław Jabłonowski, the right-hand man of Charles's grandfather, John III Sobieski, and the daughter of Jakub Sobieski's first cousin.[11] There were rumours—particularly strong in 1749—that Charles was in Poland during the nine years in which he kept his movements a closely-guarded secret following his expulsion from France in 1748. These reports have not been corroborated, but a letter from Pope Benedict XIV of 24 May 1752 reported that Charles was visiting his Radziwiłł cousins, staying at one of their country estates in Poland-Lithuania; the news prompted Empress Elizabeth of Russia to tip off George II, who urged her to expel him.[12]

James never supported the idea of either of his sons putting themselves forward as candidates for the Polish throne, while in 1748, Charles angrily dismissed a suggestion he might seek election. For a dynasty that had staked so much on its hereditary claim to the British throne, an elective crown had little appeal, while becoming king of Poland and grand duke of Lithuania would have created an insurmountable obstacle to the British throne. Charles converted to Anglicanism in 1750, which would have compromised any subsequent bid for the Polish throne, and he did not put himself forward as a candidate in 1763 after Augustus III's death, despite the fact that by this time he had no prospect of securing the British throne.[13]

Private, not public matters provide a more plausible context for the painting of a portrait of Charles in Polish dress in the 1730s. Clementina took a close and shrewd interest in family matters, both during her period of self-imposed exile in the Ursuline convent in Trastevere and after her return to the family in 1727. Her sons were very attached to her and spent time with her against the background of the considerable tension between their parents that continued until her death. Charles had just turned 14 when his mother died and was considerably affected by her loss. As a head-strong adolescent, he already had a difficult relationship with his father—whom he suspected of favouring the placid Henry—which soured considerably as Charles matured and pushed for a more robust pursuit of a Stuart restoration than his more cautious father was prepared to countenance.

[11] Piniński, Peter. 2012. *Bonnie Prince Charlie, A Life*. Stroud: Amberley, 58–60, 63–9.
[12] Piniński 2012, 133.
[13] McLynn, 2020, 326.

Clementina and James were in frequent contact with Jakub and the rest of her Polish family, and Clementina wrote regularly to her older sister, Maria Karolina (1697–1740) after her marriage to Frédéric Maurice de la Tour d'Auvergne, son of Emmanuel Théodose de la Tour d'Auvergne, Duc de Bouillon (1668–1730), in September 1723. It was not a successful match. Originally, the impoverished Emmanuel Théodose had intended to marry Maria Karolina himself, while his son would marry her older sister, Maria Casimira, to ensure that the family secured as much of the fabled Sobieski wealth in dowries as was possible. Jakub opposed the plan, however: he wanted Maria Karolina to marry her cousin, Michał Kazimierz Radziwiłł (1702–1762), known as Rybenko, who had fallen for her, and whose affection she returned. Unfortunately, however, Rybenko was engaged to a much wealthier heiress, Maria Zofia Sieniawska (1669–1771). His family opposed any breaking of the engagement and made it clear they would demand a colossal dowry as the price of any marriage. Jakub was shocked by Emmanuel Théodose's high expectations and strongly opposed the dual match. His opposition enraged his daughters, but the dual marriage plan came to nothing, as the mortified Maria Casimira died in early 1723, although Maria Karolina was eventually permitted to marry not Emmanuel Théodose, but his son, Frédéric Maurice, in September 1723.[14]

The marriage was not a success. Maria Karolina's new husband was suffering from the after-effects of a serious fall from his horse when she married him; he promptly infected his bride with smallpox and died ten days after the wedding. The la Tour d'Auvergne were determined, however, not to lose the large dowry of 750,000 livres. They persuaded Maria Karolina to marry Frédéric's younger brother, Charles-Godefroy (1706–1771), who became Duc de Bouillon on his father's death in 1730. This marriage proved as disastrous as the first, in this case because the bridegroom did not die ten days after the wedding, for the couple proved spectacularly ill-matched. The unfortunate Maria Karolina separated from her husband in the early 1730s, but the marriage did produce two children: a daughter, Marie Louise (1725–1793), who married Jules Hercule de Rohan, Prince de Guéméné and Duc de Montbazon (1726–1788) in 1743, and a son, Godefroy de la Tour d'Auvergne (1728–1792), who succeeded his father as sovereign Duc de Bouillon in 1771. Jakub was enraged, however, by this second marriage, since Maria Karolina had

---

[14] Skrzypietz, Aleksandra. 2011. *Królewscy synowie—Jakub, Aleksander i Konstanty Sobiescy.* Katowice: Wydanwnictwo Uniwersytetu Śląskiego, 560–8.

neglected to ask for his permission or even inform him of the match until after her wedding. Clementina's connivance in the arrangement—she had written to the pope to secure the necessary dispensation—meant that she fell into her father's disfavour until the birth of Henry softened his stance.[15]

Jakub had good reason to be angry. Maria Karolina's second marriage created a new set of problems for the Stuarts in the long saga of the struggle for the Sobieski riches, which Jakub was keen that his grandsons should inherit. For there was one fundamental issue that had to be faced before that could happen: the requirement under Polish law that heirs should possess Polish citizenship—*indygenat* as it was termed—before they could inherit landed estates in Poland or Lithuania. Anticipating the problem, Clementina and James had long been urging Jakub to take action on behalf of his grandsons. Jakub lobbied the Polish-Lithuanian Sejm (parliament) to secure recognition of their rights. He even wrote to Anna, Empress of Russia, asking for her support. In both cases, he was unsuccessful.[16]

It is no accident that Jakub began to seek this recognition in 1735. For Clementina's death in January of that year changed a great deal, and left the Stuarts vulnerable. As things stood, Maria Karolina—to whom Maria Casimira had left all her property on her death in 1723—could inherit the vast Sobieski estates in Poland-Lithuania, but James's sons could not. The stakes were high. As the size of the Bouillon dowry demonstrates, the Sobieskis were—or at least were thought to be—fabulously wealthy. Jakub Sobieski was no ordinary Polish nobleman. His father had been grand hetman—one of the two commanders of the Polish army—before his election to the throne, achieved on a frenzied wave of support after his crushing victory over the Ottomans at the battle of Khotyn (Chocim) in 1673. Hetmans had substantial powers over the recruitment, payment, and stationing of the army, which furnished them with ample opportunities to make money. Few hetmans died poor, and John Sobieski was already a rich man when elected to the throne in 1674. He lent money to the Polish-Lithuanian republic, and part of the Polish crown jewels were pawned to him during his reign in return for a loan that the republic could not repay. For a quarter of a century, Sobieski used his position as king to enrich his family and establish it as one of the leading magnate families in the Polish-Lithuanian Commonwealth.

[15] Skrzypietz 2011, 569–70; Skrzypietz 2015, 332.
[16] Skrzypietz 2011, 584.

Despite Jakub's failure to secure election to the throne in 1697, the Sobieski fortune was considerable: at Jakub's death in 1737, his estates comprised 11 towns and 140 villages, each with a landed estate attached to it: apart from the great complex of lands in Poland's Ruthenian territories—mostly in what is now western Ukraine—he owned lucrative properties near Danzig and held a mortgage on the substantial royal estate of Szawle (Šiauliai), in Lithuania, one of the wealthiest in the Commonwealth. The Sobieski estates, however, had been divided between Jakub and his two brothers, Aleksander (1677–1714) and Konstanty (1680–1726) in 1697. Although some consolidation took place following Aleksander's death in 1714, they had suffered considerable devastation during the Great Northern War and were loaded with debt. Thus, as the Stuarts soon discovered, although the 1719 dowry agreement looked enticing on paper, realising its riches was an entirely different matter.[17]

More seriously, the Stuarts were not the only potential heirs. After the death of Konstanty, the youngest brother, in 1726, Jakub became involved in a property dispute with Konstanty's wife, Maria Józefa Wessel, whom Konstanty had married in 1708 against the wishes of his French mother, the dowager queen, Marie Casimire Sobieska (1641–1716), known as Marysieńka. There were no children and a divorce settlement was agreed in 1711, but Maria Józefa repudiated it after her mother-in-law's death. Haggling over a settlement dragged on until Konstanty's death, while Maria Józefa began selling off some of the family assets. It was only in 1728 that agreement was reached. Konstanty in the interim had sold the Sobieski estates of Podhorce and Wilanów, and it was not until 1728 that Maria Józefa moved out of the main Sobieski palace at Żółkiew, now Zhovkva in Ukraine. Jakub finally had full possession of what was left of his father's lands, which raised the value of the potential inheritance for the Stuarts considerably, but he became increasingly lonely and depressed. Living on his Silesian estates, his melancholy was not improved by a complex dispute with Charles VI over loans he had made to the Austrian government which had not been repaid. In 1734 he left Ohlau for good, expelled by Charles, to take up residence at Żółkiew. The move did not help: he was surrounded by too many paintings and mementoes of his

---

[17] Skrzypietz 2015, 315–6.

father's triumphs, which only served to highlight his own failures. Vague plans to write a history of the family came to nothing.[18]

From the mid-1720s, James and Clementina became increasingly concerned about the Sobieski inheritance. Clementina had long been urging her father to sell the family estates and move to Italy. This option would remove the problem of citizenship and open the way to a clear settlement of the inheritance issue, which was complicated when Jakub fell out with Maria Karolina over her second marriage. Responding angrily to her disobedience, he cut her out of his will in 1726, after failing to persuade her to renounce all claims to the Sobieski inheritance. Characteristically obsessed with the family's status, he stipulated that she should not appear at Versailles unless permitted to stand among the princes of the blood royal.[19] The exclusion of Maria Karolina from his will meant that in the event of a sale of the Sobieski estates, James's sons stood to inherit all the proceeds.[20]

There were many difficulties to be overcome before that goal could be reached, however. Clementina, who showed a shrewd grasp of financial matters, was keen both to see her father and to secure a settlement for her sons. In 1730, she took the initiative, urging her father to sell his Polish estates—tentative negotiations had already opened with the Radziwiłłs—which would enable him to place the proceeds safely in a Dutch bank, move to Italy, and buy property there. She even had a suggestion with regard to the property he might buy: Monte Rotondo in Rome, the offer price for which she regarded as a good deal.[21] Once the Sobieski wealth was relocated from Poland to Italy, the question of Polish citizenship would no longer arise, and her father could bequeath his property to his grandsons without problem.

Nothing came of the idea, however. The congenitally indecisive Jakub responded to James and Clementina's urgings by suggesting that James should instead move to Poland, something that his son-in-law would never countenance. Clementina's death in January 1735 complicated

---

[18] Skrzypietz 2011, 576–8, 583. For the artistic strategy of the Sobieski family in Żółkiew, see Jagodzinski, Sabine. 2013. *Die Türkenkriege im Spiegel der polnisch-litauischen Adelskultur. Kommemoration und Repräntation bei den Żółkiewski, Sobieski und Radziwiłł.* Studia Jagiellonica Lipsiensia Bd 13. Ostfildern: Jan Thorbecke Verlag.

[19] Skrzypietz 2015, 330.

[20] Skrzypietz 2011, 571.

[21] Clementina to Jakub Sobieski, 28 January, 4 February, and 20 May 1730, *Sobiesciana.* 1882, 22, nos. 100–2.

matters further. James had to proceed cautiously. He had devoted careful attention to maintaining good relations with his father-in-law, for whom he had considerable sympathy, although they had never met. The two men understood each other. They were both neurotically sensitive to the slights they received on account of not having followed their fathers onto their respective thrones; in Jakub's case, the sensitivity was particularly acute due to the condescension with which hereditary monarchs regarded the son of an elected monarch neither of whom had been born royal. Although the sons of their elected monarchs were given the courtesy title of *królewicz*, Polish law banned any treatment of them as heirs to the throne, and the strong culture of egalitarianism among the *szlachta* meant that they were treated like any other nobleman. Thus, like James, Jakub insisted on the title of His Royal Highness (*Jego Królewska Wysokość*) and refused to answer correspondence in which he was not properly addressed.[22]

James's antennae were well attuned to the sour sense of entitlement of the dispossessed, and his correspondence with Jakub was frequent and often warm, although they did have their disagreements. In the early 1730s James kept Jakub closely informed of Clementina's worsening health and wrote a long, touching letter of condolence to him after her death.[23] Anxious to arrange matters before Jakub died, in October 1735 James wrote expressing his concern that the campaign for citizenship was unlikely to succeed and urging Jakub to sell his estates as soon as possible if he wanted his Stuart grandsons to inherit, using the proceeds either to buy Monte Rotondo or to invest in the Monte di Pietà, where they would be safer.[24]

Clementina's death created new difficulties. As a concerned letter from James pointed out, Jakub's testamentary dispositions were far from clear: among Clementina's papers were no fewer than six versions of Jakub's will. James was concerned that his father-in-law's disinheritance of Maria Karolina might not be legally valid. Moreover, there was no reference to the jewels pawned in the Monte di Pietà in any of the drafts.[25] Given the problem of *indygenat*, the failure to sell the Polish estates opened up the real possibility that Charles and Henry would end up with nothing if

---

[22] Skrzypietz 2015, 7–8; Libiszowska, Zofia. 1980. Ród Sobieskich w Europie po śmierci Jana III, *Sobótka* 35/2, 359–60.

[23] James to Jakub Sobieski, 21 January 1735, AGAD, Warsaw, AR, dz. III, 276, 41–7; copy in RA SP/MAIN/, 177/31.

[24] James to Jakub Sobieski, 1 & 28 October 1735, *Sobiesciana*. 1883, 28, nos. 133, 134.

[25] James to Jakub Sobieski, Rome, 29 July 1735, *Sobiesciana* 1883, 27–8, no. 131.

Jakub died before selling-up or making a new will, as James made clear in another anxious letter he wrote to Maria Karolina in April 1736, in which he baldly stated that although he had a copy of Jakub's will, Clementina's death had rendered it invalid. He hoped that Jakub would draw up a new one, but if he died intestate, his estate would be shared between Maria Karolina and the two Stuart princes.[26] His care in stressing the rights of his sons indicates his real concern that on account of the problem over citizenship, which he mentioned in the letter, they might end up with nothing.

James was certainly anxious about Jakub's intentions with regard to Maria Karolina and her children, but he sensibly had no wish to become involved in a struggle with his sister-in-law over the Sobieski inheritance, which might be highly damaging to his sons' prospects. Clementina had sought to effect a reconciliation between her sister and her father before her death, and Maria Karolina, after the shattering of her marriage, travelled to Poland with the same end in mind. Her father spurned her when she first arrived in Żółkiew, but she took up residence in Jarosław, not far away, and played a patient game. Her son, Godefroy, had been left behind in France, but her estranged husband allowed her daughter, Marie Louise, to join her. In the end, Maria Karolina's patience was rewarded, and Jakub's frosty demeanour began to soften. In early 1736 she moved to Żółkiew to be with her father, who came to dote on Marie Louise, the only one of his four grandchildren he ever met; he even began to badger James about marrying her off to one of the Stuart princes, which might simplify the problems of inheritance. James was sceptical, and as Skrzypietz points out, the princes would still have counted as foreigners, unable to inherit.[27]

James was in a delicate position. He continued his pressure on Jakub to effect a rapid sale, but was clearly concerned about Maria Karolina's presence in Poland: in a letter of 28 October 1735 he asked anxiously about a passage in one of Jakub's letters concerning his father-in-law's intentions with regard to the inheritance of Maria Karolina's children.[28] Yet James could not afford to alienate Maria Karolina, who would inherit the Polish estates if Jakub died intestate, meaning that his sons might have to rely on

[26] James to Maria Karolina, duchess of Bouillon, 7 April 1736, *Sobiesciana*. 1883, 28–9, no. 136.

[27] Skrzypietz 2015, 376.

[28] James to Jakub Sobieski, Rome, 28 October 1735, *Sobiesciana*. 1883, 28, no. 134.

her good nature to receive anything at all that they had not already inherited from their mother which, given the uncertainty over the ownership of the jewels lodged in the Monte di Pietà, might be open to challenge. James had therefore supported Clementina's efforts to secure a reconciliation between Jakub and Maria Karolina and sought to effect one after his wife's death. He wrote to Jakub as early as 1733 urging him to restore Maria Karolina to his affections and repeated the sentiment in January 1735.[29] In his April 1736 letter to Maria Karolina, he assured her that all he had ever sought was a reconciliation with her father.[30]

In the end, James's prudent campaign brought dividends. A sensible agreement was reached over the division of the spoils before Jakub's death on 19 December 1737. Jakub left the income from the Ohlau estate and the Sobieski jewels to his Stuart grandsons; since Ohlau was located in the Empire, and the jewels were safely lodged in the Monte di Pietà, the citizenship issue did not arise. The Polish estates and Sobieski money located outside Poland-Lithuania were to be held in trust for Marie-Louise Maria Karolina's daughter: she would inherit them on her marriage. If she did not marry, they would be sold off, and the proceeds would be distributed among Jakub's other descendants.

In the event, the Polish estates were so encumbered with debt that Maria Karolina sold them to Rybenko, her cousin and former admirer shortly before her death.[31] Charles and Henry were to receive part of the proceeds, but there were problems over Ohlau. Maria Karolina intended to live there and ordered that the doors be sealed on her father's death. Her intention was to fight for the money owed to Jakub by the Habsburgs, but she was refused permission to live there by her cousin, Charles VI, and her efforts, strongly supported by James, came to nothing.[32] In the event, the original agreement with Rybenko, dated 30 November 1739, in which Maria Karolina was accorded residency rights on her father's Żółkiew estate and a million złoties, from which she was to settle the claims of the Stuarts, had to be renegotiated on account of the problems posed by the immense debts accumulated by Jakub, as his creditors began petitioning. Stuart interests were represented by Jan Tarło, palatine of Sandomierz, and Jan

---

[29] James to Jakub Sobieski, Rome, 1 May 1733 and 7 January 1735, *Sobiesciana*. 1883, 26, 28, nos. 123, 135.
[30] James to Maria Karolina, 7 April 1736, *Sobiesciana*. 1883, 29, no. 136.
[31] Skrzypietz 2011, 587–8.
[32] Skrzypietz 2011, 588–9.

Kajetan Jabłonowski, starosta of Czehryń and brother of Charles Edward's future mistress, the princess of Talmont, but James was not always pleased with their efforts on his behalf.[33] A second agreement was signed on 11 March 1740, which was rather less favourable to Maria Karolina.[34]

The agreement did not resolve the uncertainty over the Stuart share of the inheritance. Maria Karolina's death in Żółkiew on 8 May 1740, a couple of months after the agreement was signed, meant that nothing was resolved, and James entered into a lengthy correspondence with Rybenko. He was concerned to ensure that his sons secured their due, while ensuring that the Stuarts accepted no liability for settling Jakub's debts.[35] Tortuous negotiations over the next two years produced an agreement with Rybenko, but Tarło had his own claims on the Sobieski estate, and James repudiated an agreement he made on the matter with Jabłonowski, which James considered to be detrimental to the interests of his sons.[36] By November the matter had been settled, and James told Rybenko that he now regarded him as the true heir of the house of Sobieski in Poland, although Tarło was still pressing his case.[37]

It is not clear what share the Stuarts received of the Sobieski millions, apart from the jewels safely lodged in Italy. They were already involved in what proved to be a long and bitter dispute with the la Tour d'Auvergne family, which fought long and hard for the rights of Godefroy, Maria Karolina's son, who had been excluded from the cosy deal agreed between James and Maria Karolina. This dispute rumbled on for decades: among Henry's papers is a considerable stack of legal documents and correspondence charting its intricate course, and documenting the activities of Tarło and Jabłonowski, who continued to fight their cause in the Polish and Lithuanian courts.[38] To determine what benefit the Stuarts derived from their efforts is a research project for another day.

---

[33] James to Maria Karolina, Rome, 1.III.1740, AGAD, AR dz. III, 277, 10–12.

[34] Skrzypietz, Aleksandra. 2003. Maria Karolina de Bouillon i jej kontakty z Radziwiłłami. In Stępnik, Krzysztof, ed. *Radziwiłłowie. Obrazy literackie. Biografie. Świadectwa historyczne.* Lublin: Wydawnictwo Uniwersytetu Marii Curie-Skłodowskiej, 375–7.

[35] James to Rybenko, Rome, 26.III.1740, AGAD, AR dz. III, 277, 14–16.

[36] James to Jan Kajetan Jabłonowski, Rome, 16.II.1742, AGAD, AR dz. III, 277, 40–2.

[37] James to Rybenko, Rome, 17.XI.1742, AGAD, AR dz. III, 277, 46–7; James to Rybenko, Rome, 16.III.1743, AGAD, AR dz. III, 277, 52–3.

[38] BL, Add Ms 30477. The file includes inventories of Clementina's jewels and other property, documents, and correspondence in Latin, French, Italian, and Polish, and a long Italian summary drawn up for Henry (ff. 65–103) of all the property disputes surrounding the Sobieski inheritance.

BIBLIOGRAPHY

SECONDARY SOURCES

Corp, Edward. 2011. *The Stuarts in Italy 1719–1766. A Royal Court in Permanent Exile*. Cambridge: Cambridge University Press.

Farquhar, Helen. 1923–1924. Some portrait medals struck between 1745 and 1752 for Prince Charles Edward. *British Numismatic Journal* 17, 171–225.

McLynn, Frank. 2020. *Bonnie Prince Charlie: Charles Edward Stuart*. London: Sharpe Books.

Piniński, Peter. 2012. *Bonnie Prince Charlie, A Life*. Stroud: Amberley.

Shield, Alice. 1908. *Henry Stuart, Cardinal of York*. London: Longmans, Green & Co.

Skrzypietz, Aleksandra. 2015. *Jakub Sobieski*. Poznań: Wydawnictwo Poznańskie.

Skrzypietz, Aleksandra. 2011. *Królewscy synowie—Jakub, Aleksander i Konstanty Sobiescy*. Katowice: Wydanwnictwo Uniwersytetu Śląskiego.

CHAPTER 5

Portraits for the Sobieskis

Abstract This chapter examines the role played by art in relations between the Stuarts and the Sobieskis. It presents two portraits of the infant Prince Charles in Polish dress commissioned by Clementina Sobieska that provide possible precedents for the NPG portrait, and discusses her artistic strategies.

Keywords Clementina Sobieska • Stuart-Sobieski relations • Bonnie Prince Charlie portraits • Sobieski inheritance • Jakub Sobieski • James III and VIII

Art played its part in this complex round of family diplomacy. That is hardly surprising, since art was one of the primary ways in which the Stuarts sought to influence opinion and remind a European-wide audience of their position and status. During the 1730s, James cranked up the Stuart propaganda machine as Charles reached the verge of adulthood. James was relatively well off after the new pope, Clement XII, elected in 1730, proved more supportive than his predecessor, Benedict XIII, increasing James's papal pension and allowing Henry to hold ecclesiastical benefices before he had reached the age prescribed by canon law.[1] James's revived finances ensured that he was able to mount a new propaganda

[1] Corp 2011, 213–25.

campaign in favour of the young princes, central to which was the commissioning of the great portraits by David, Liotard, and Blanchet, and the distribution of numerous engravings of them: in September 1736 Baron Philipp von Stosch (1691–1757), a Hanoverian agent who kept a close eye on the Stuart court, noted that James was sending a large number of painted portraits of Charles to England.[2]

It would be surprising if a similar strategy had not been adopted with regard to the important family issues at stake in Poland-Lithuania. Portraits had long played a part in Sobieski-Stuart relations. Despite Clementina's heartfelt entreaties, Jakub never visited Rome and never saw his Stuart grandsons. He took a close interest in them, however, and was frequently sent news of their activities, as well as dutiful if uninspiring letters written by the young princes themselves.[3] He was as interested as any grandparent in what they looked like, and Clementina launched her own artistic campaign during her two-year exile from the family to ensure that he received pictures of them. David's bill of 1727 reveals that Clementina had commissioned from him a full-length portrait "of the little Duke"—that is Henry—"to be sent to her father, the Most Serene Prince James (Jakub Sobieski)", which David was to charge to her husband's account. He did, and James refused to pay.[4] Thus, while separated from James, Clementina was commissioning paintings and billing them to her husband; as Corp remarks, this has caused considerable confusion for historians of Stuart portraiture following the production of a number of inferior copies, and a lack of clarity about what pictures were painted and which have survived.[5]

There are two striking images of Charles dating from precisely this period which prove that there are precedents for the Polish portrait, indicate that Clementina was keen to establish an image of her sons as Poles, and suggest that she may have had a future bid for the Polish throne in mind, or was already considering the problem of citizenship. In his catalogue, under the reproduction of the Polish portrait, without the

[2] Gregg, Edward. 2003. The financial vicissitudes of James III in Rome. In Corp, Edward & Fowle, Francis, eds. *The Stuart Court in Rome. The Legacy of Exile.* Aldershot: Ashgate, 74–6.

[3] See, for example, the letters from Charles to Jakub of 1732, 1734, 1735, and 1737 in AGAD, AR 249.

[4] Wortley, Clara Stuart. 1948. Data from the Stuart Papers at Windsor dealing with the Portraits of the Royal Stuarts. Prepared by the Hon. Clara Stuart Wortley and edited, after her death, by Henrietta Tayler. 1948: Heinz Archive, NPG, section ii, 17.

[5] Corp 2001, 64.

slightest comment, Nicholas prints a grainy picture of a miniature of a child with the caption: "Catherine Sperlingin/Prince Charles as a child in Polish dress, signed and dated 1726 3³/₄ high/ Messers Christie, Manson & Woods".[6] Nicholas gives no further information, and Stuart historians have shown no interest in the image. Nicholson does not list it in his catalogue of portraits of Charles Edward, and neither he nor Corp mentions Heckel-Sperling. A watercolour and gouache painting on parchment, it was sold by Willy Muller at Christie's in London on 28 October 1970 (lot 104) and was bought for 224 guineas by someone named Conway.[7] The painting is now in the Tansey Miniatures Foundation collection in Celle (Fig. 5.1).[8]

It is signed in the bottom left corner: *Cathar: Sperlingin. geb. Hecklin./ pinx: Aug: Vind: 1726*. Catherina Sperling, Sperlingen, or Heckel-Sperling was born Catherina Heckel in Augsburg in 1699. Not much is known about her. A childhood prodigy who was producing engravings at the age of 12, she was taught drawing by her silversmith father, Michael Heckel (c. 1656–1722), and engraving by Johann Ulrich Kraus in Nuremberg. In 1725 she married another Kraus student, the engraver Hieronymus Sperling (1695–1777), and produced several fine engravings of biblical scenes and landscapes of Italy, where she was active in the 1720s, although she returned to Germany, working between 1731 and 1735 with Johann Andreas Pfeffel on the engravings for Johann Jacob Scheuchzer's *Physica Sacra* back in Augsburg, where she died in 1741. Another miniature of Charles as a child in western dress, painted around 1728 and also attributed to Heckel-Sperling was in the L.H. Gilbert Collection, Lisbon, until 1963, when it was sold at Christie's London on 3 December 1963, and was in the Albion Collection, London, until 2004, when it was sold at auction by Bonhams in London (lot 19) on 24 April 2004 for $26,529.[9]

[6] Nicholas 1973, 46.

[7] I am grateful to Jo Langston of Christies for supplying information about the sale, and the image from the sale catalogue. The catalogue description reads: "PRINCE CHARLES EDWARD STUART, the Young Pretender 'Bonnie Prince Charlie' as a child, by *Catherine Sperlingin, signed and dated* 1726, standing in a wooded landscape dressed in scarlet with fur-trimmed cloak and hat, and a scarlet cane on his left arm—rectangular, 3¾ in. (99 cm.) *high*—in turned wood frame. *The young Prince was probably dressed in Polish costume because his mother, Clementina Sobieska, was a Polish Princess*".

[8] Charles Edward Stuart by Catharina Sperling, née Hackel, 1726. http://tansey-miniatures.com/en/collection/#/10658, accessed 28 July 2016.

[9] https://www.auctionclub.com/public/historic/attributed-to%2D%2Dcatharina-sperling-heckel-33943/prince-charles-edward-stuart-the-young-pretender-33150/ and

Fig. 5.1 Prince Charles Edward Stuart by Catherina Heckel-Sperling (1726). Tansey Miniatures Foundation 10658. (Photo by Birgitt Schmedding)

http://www.blouinartinfo.com/artists/catharina-sperling-heckel-173481, accessed 28 July 2016. Pappe, Bernd & Schmieglitz-Otten, Juliane. 2008. *Miniaturen des Rokoko aus der Sammlung Tansey*, 230. Munich: Hirmer Verlag; Schmidt-Liebich, Jochen. 2005. *Lexikon Der Kunstlerinnen 1700–1900. Deutschland, Österreich, Schweiz.* Berlin: De Gruyter Saur, 184–5.

Since Heckel-Sperling's miniature is dated August 1726, it is assumed by scholars that she was present at James's court in Bologna and that he commissioned it. This seems unlikely. Apart from the fact that the court did not move to Bologna until September 1726, why would James have commissioned a painting of his son in Polish dress at the height of his quarrel with Clementina? It is far more likely that it was Clementina who commissioned it. It would have been a symbolic act of defiance to have her son depicted in Polish dress to remind her husband that she herself was the granddaughter of a king and to emphasise Charles's Polish identity in the context of the breakdown of her relationship with James, in which the question of her status played the central role. There are distinct similarities to the costume worn in the Polish portrait: the sitter wears a fur-lined cloak held by a small chain over a bound with a belt. He sports a Polish-style sabre and a plumed hat.

Thus, Clementina had her own artistic strategy, set up in opposition to that of her husband. She was certainly commissioning portraits during her estrangement from her husband. Sir William Ellis wrote to James in April 1727:

> Card. Gualtierio sent word to lett me know [that the] Queen complains of her Maties being ill-used on acct of a Picture which her Matie says y[ou]r Matie allowed she should have done which I refused to pay for, and she, so the Cardinal said, if it was a matter of 5 pistoles His Eminence wd take on him to order me to pay it. I ans^rd there were several pictures in David's bill bespoke by [the] Queen wh[ich] I could not pay for and particularly one for which David demanded forty Span. Pistoles—it is a picture of [the] Prince. I sent the bill to Bologna and I ordered Mr Belloni to pay all those in s[ai]d bill wh[ich]. My Lord Inverness [John Hay] marked as allowed by yr Matie.[10]

Altogether, the queen commissioned five portraits from David.[11] If James was unwilling to pay, then Clementina would have been unable to afford to engage David himself, or another artist of his quality. It can only be the queen who commissioned Heckel-Sperling.

One of the pictures mentioned by Ellis was probably another depiction of the Prince in Polish dress. Identified as the work of Antonio David, it was sold by the Dorotheum auction-house in Vienna on 16 October 2007

---

[10] RA SP/MAIN/, 106/12.
[11] Corp 2011, 117.

Fig. 5.2   Prince Charles Edward Stuart attr. Antonio David (c. 1727/8). Private Collection. (Photo Credit: Dorotheum Vienna, auction catalogue 16.10.2007)

for 24,365 euros (Fig. 5.2).[12] This painting, unlike the Heckel-Sperling portrait, is not a miniature: it measures 61 cm by 78 cm. As in the Polish portrait, Charles is wearing a *bekiesza*; as in both the Polish portrait and the Sperling miniature, there is a lack of royal imagery, but the King Charles spaniel indicates the subject's identity. Finally, in the light of the discussion in Chap. 3 of the shape of the princely countenance, it might be

[12] Information from Artnet.com: https://www.artnet.com/PDB/FAADSearch/LotDetail View.aspx?Page=1&artType=FineArt&subTypeId=307. Accessed 2 October 2016. The reserve price listed in the catalogue was 12–16,000 euros.

noted that David portrays Charles with the rounded cheeks of a child, in stark contrast to the idealised image he painted for James in 1729, in which he was instructed to paint the prince much older than he was in reality. If the Polish portrait was done from life, then it is possible that it shows Charles in the process of losing the puppy fat that he clearly carries in David's depiction of him in Polish dress.

Once Clementina returned to her family following her formal reconciliation with James in Bologna in January 1728, it was important for James to restore good relations with her family, and portraits once more played their part. In April 1728, when Clementina was experiencing what proved to be a phantom pregnancy, he wrote to Jakub that she was expecting a boy and that he would be named James (Jakub) after his father and grandfather.[13] James wrote on his return to Bologna that he was "daily expecting" a famous painter, by which he meant David, adding that he would send portraits of both his sons to Jakub; in June he wrote again, assuring Jakub that he was expecting a "very good painter" any day.[14] In 1729 Clementina wrote that she was delighted with the latest portraits of the two and wished that he could see them.[15]

In February 1735, a month after Clementina's death, James was planning to send new portraits to Jakub. In a postscript to a letter written to his father-in-law in February, James stated that two good portraits of his sons had been completed, which he would have reproduced in miniature, as Jakub had requested, and would have sent as soon as possible.[16] In July he expressed his hope that they might be sent through Fr Jacques Costa, who was soon to travel to Lwów.[17] It is likely that these were copies of David's reworking of his 1729 portrait, which were completed in the winter of 1734–1735.[18]

---

[13] James to Jakub Sobieski, Bologna, 4 April 1728, *Sobiesciana*. 1883. 20, no. 87.

[14] Wortley suggests that this was the Bologna painter Stefano Torelli (1712–1784): Data, section ii, 25, but in fact James was referring to Giovanna Fratellini, having previously employed Lucia Casalini Torelli; the paintings by both artists have all been lost: Corp 2001, 108.

[15] Clementina to Jakub Sobieski, Rome, 8 June 1729, *Sobiesciana*. 1883, 21, no. 97.

[16] "On vient d'achever les Portraits de mes Enfans, qui sont assez bien faits. Je les ferai copier en petit comme vous avez desiré, et vous les enverrai au plutôt". James to Jakub Sobieski, Albano, 12 February 1735, AGAD, AR dz. III, 276, 52.

[17] James to Jakub Sobieski, 23 July 1735, AGAD, AR, dz. III, 276, 53.

[18] Corp 2001, 70.

It was not just Jakub who received portraits of the young princes. In his letter of April 1736 to Maria Karolina, in which he expressed his concern that Jakub's will had been invalidated by Clementina's death, James promised to send her portraits of his sons once his personal painter had returned from Naples, adding that the same artist had already painted portraits of them which had been sent to Jakub.[19] The artist referred to is David, who had left the court in 1735, and was in Naples in April 1736, but who never returned before his death in 1737.[20] Finally, in a letter of October 1736 written to congratulate Jakub on his upcoming birthday, James wrote that he had in his hands the reliquary with a fragment of the True Cross that Jakub had asked for, which he promised to send him at the earliest opportunity, together with the portraits of the princes for Maria Karolina.[21]

Thus, there is evidence of four separate portraits commissioned for the Sobieski family at precisely the period that the Polish portrait, if it is genuine, must have been painted. The two miniatures by David were indeed sent to Jakub—presumably through Father Costa—but it is not clear what transpired with regard to the two that James was planning to have painted for Maria Karolina who, by April 1736, was resident in Żółkiew with her father, not least since David did not return as James had expected he would when he wrote. As Corp states, at this point, after Clementina's death, "the story of Stuart portraiture becomes even more complicated", with no new images painted until 1737, when Liotard and Blanchet were commissioned to paint them, although still on the basis of a much younger face for Charles.[22]

Were the pictures for Maria Karolina ever painted? James's suggestion in his letter of 5 October 1736 that he would send the portraits to Maria Karolina "at the earliest opportunity" suggests that he had given up waiting for David's return from Naples. Liotard's portrait was finished in December 1737, the month that Jakub died; copies were sent in 1738 to Vienna, to the dowager Duchess of Parma, with several despatched to England and France. Maria Karolina was in Poland, and there is no record

---

[19] James to Maria Karolina, 7 April 1736, *Sobiesciana*. 1883, 29, no. 136.

[20] It is widely claimed that David died in 1750, but it is known from a letter of Charles, King of the Two Sicilies, that he died in 1737: Corp 2011, 286.

[21] "J'ai entre mes mains la Relique de la Ste Croix que vous avez souhaité pour vous etre envoyée par la premiere bonne occasion, avec les Portraits de mes Enfants pour ma Belle Soeur, a laquelle Je vous prie de faire mes tendres compliments". James to Jakub Sobieski, 5 October 1736, AGAD, AR, dz. III, 276, 58.

[22] Corp 2001, 72.

that she was sent copies. By 1738, Jakub's death had transformed the context: an agreement had been reached with Maria Karolina over Jakub's testament, and the need was no longer so pressing.

Given the complex family politics surrounding the Sobieski inheritance following Clementina's death, there would be good reason to have Charles painted in Polish dress in 1736–1737, before agreement was reached over the Sobieski estates. Whatever the prospects for the princes being granted Polish citizenship, until the Polish estates were sold, there was every reason to remind a Polish audience of their Polish descent, while there was also a good private reason for so doing at a time when Maria Karolina's daughter, Marie-Louise was charming her grandfather in Żółkiew. For such an audience, the usual Stuart iconography, with the emphasis on the orders of the Garter and the Thistle, would have meant nothing; indeed, it might well have been damaging in the light of the negative attitude of the egalitarian Polish nobility to chivalric orders. For a Polish audience it would be better to avoid the orders altogether and rely on a rich ermine robe to emphasise the sitter's princely status.

BIBLIOGRAPHY

SECONDARY SOURCES

Corp, Edward. 2001. *The King over the Water. Portraits of the Stuarts in Exile after 1689*. Edinburgh: Scottish National Portrait Gallery.
Corp, Edward. 2011. *The Stuarts in Italy 1719–1766. A Royal Court in Permanent Exile*. Cambridge: Cambridge University Press.
Nicholas, Donald. 1973. *The Portraits of Bonnie Prince Charlie*. Maidstone: Clout & Baker.

CHAPTER 6

Unknown Man; Unknown Artist

Abstract This chapter considers the problem of when, if the portrait is genuine, it might have been painted, by whom, and under what circumstances. In particular, it looks at the case for and against Pompeo Batoni, the most fashionable portrait painter in Rome from the 1740s, who was drawing tutor to Charles Edward and his brother in the 1730s.

Keywords Pompeo Batoni • Stuart artefacts • Charles Edward Stuart • James III and VIII • Polish portrait, authenticity

So if a reasonably plausible case can be constructed to explain why a portrait from life of Charles in Polish dress might have been painted, when might it have been painted, and who might have painted it? If it is genuine, the Polish portrait, judging by the age of the sitter and the fact that he is depicted with his own hair, must have been painted before the famous episode in August 1737 when Charles's hair was ceremoniously cut off.[1] At precisely this point, another artist enters the frame. From the 1750s, British aristocrats on the Grand Tour flocked to Rome to have their portraits painted by Pompeo Batoni (1708–1787), from about 1750 the most fashionable portrait-painter in Europe. In the 1730s,

---

[1] RA SP/MAIN/, 199/166. McLynn 2020, 49–50.

however, Batoni was merely a determined and ambitious young artist on the make. He had developed considerable skill as a draughtsman in his native Lucca, where his father was a renowned goldsmith, but had taken instruction in painting against his father's wishes. In 1727 he left Lucca for Rome, where his talent brought him to the attention of local artistic circles. He developed his reputation painting altarpieces in collaboration with his mentor, Francesco Fernandi (1679–1740), known as Imperiali. Batoni's first commission came in 1732 for an altarpiece in the Gabrielli family chapel in the Camadolese monastery church of San Gregorio al Celio; he then painted a large allegorical canvas, *The Triumph of Venice* for Marco Foscarini, Venetian ambassador to the Holy See (1737).[2]

Batoni's reputation as a portraitist was firmly based on his skill as a draughtsman. He was still learning his trade in the 1730s, however. He had not yet begun to work as a portrait painter, and it was on account of his skill as a draughtsman that he was engaged by James in the mid-1730s to teach drawing to the young princes. It is at least plausible therefore, that, with David in Naples, James might have allowed the ambitious Batoni to paint a portrait of one or both of the princes, perhaps with the intention of emphasising Charles's credentials as a Pole in the light of James's reluctance with regard to the idea that his sons should become Polish citizens, as part of a bid to assert their rights to inherit Jakub's Polish estates.

It is out of the question, however, that James commissioned Batoni to paint Charles. He was exceptionally fastidious with regard to the artists he engaged, and his commissions are minutely accounted for in the Stuart Papers. Moreover, at this point, Batoni had no body of portraits to suggest the talent he was later to display. Batoni was ambitious, however. Might he, aware that David was not coming back from Naples, and keen to use the opportunity provided by his employment by one of the major commissioners of portraits in contemporary Rome, have painted a portrait on his own initiative, recognising the potential for his career if it was a success?

Batoni might conceivably have received encouragement from another quarter. By 1736–1737, Charles's relations with James had reached a low point, as the young prince began to display the headstrong stubbornness

[2] Clark, Anthony. 1985. *Pompeo Batoni. A Complete Catalogue of his Works with an Introductory Text* ed. Bowron, Edgar Peters. Oxford: Phaidon, 15–16, 23–4. Bowron, Edgar Peters & Kerber, Peter Björn. 2007. *Pompeo Batoni. Prince of Painters in Eighteenth-Century Rome.* New Haven & London: Yale University Press, 1–3, 37.

that was to mark his career, and a love of pleasure that appalled his dull, conscientious father. James, whose marked favouring of the more dutiful Henry had already piqued Charles's resentment, was appalled at reports of Charles's behaviour on his tour of northern Italy in the spring and early summer of 1737 sent back to him by Dunbar, who was accompanying the Prince. James admonished his son in several carping, critical letters throughout what had been for the 16-year-old Charles, a liberating excursion. As the portraits he commissioned suggest, James still treated Charles as a child, writing in early 1737 that he was "very innocent and extreme backwards in some respects for his age", and expressing his hope that his trip to north Italy would "wean him away from little childish amusements and help to make him more manly".[3]

What James regarded as "more manly" is unclear; he seems to have regarded his son's increasing unwillingness to be shackled by the restraints put on his behaviour in the stuffy atmosphere of the highly-regulated Rome court as "childish". Released from his father's suffocating oversight, Charles blossomed on his tour, but not in the way James, or Pope Clement XII, who subsidised it, might have wished. At a series of balls and galas, Charles began to exhibit the alluring charm which his father so singularly lacked and to experience his notorious attractive power over women. Dunbar was unable to exert control, as the Prince's aristocratic and princely hosts issued invitations and Charles ignored his tutor's fussy attempts to constrain him. Dunbar's reports elicited a series of alarmed letters from James deprecating Charles's behaviour in a tone that, as McLynn observes, was "at best patronising and at worst downright insulting". At the end of July, before Charles returned, James wrote of his intention of cutting off his hair, an act that he suspected might displease his son.[4]

McLynn reads much psychological significance into this decision, presenting it as a symbolic gelding in which Charles had to be castrated and deprived of his power.[5] This Freudian interpretation seems overblown, led by theory rather than evidence: McLynn has to explain away a report from James Edgar, James's private secretary, who was present at the ceremony, and who wrote that Charles was delighted at this eighteenth-century rite of passage into manhood, not least because his hair was proving tiresome to manage. Edgar's account is borne out by a report of Charles having to

[3] James to O'Rourke, 9 February 1737. RA SP/MAIN/ 194/33.
[4] McLynn 2020, 48, 49.
[5] McLynn 2020, 49–50.

request that an Irish officer who saw him one morning in curl-papers during his north Italian tour should not report the matter in Dublin, as it might be misunderstood.[6]

It seems more likely that Charles welcomed the cutting of his hair and the putting-on of his wig, which Edgar thought suited him well; he was shaved for the first time in on his seventeenth birthday on the last day of 1737.[7] Charles was entering the adult world, and the donning for the first time of the elegant wigs that adorn his adult portraits symbolised his liberation rather than his gelding. As discussed in Chap. 3, while James was still commissioning childlike portraits from Liotard and Blanchet as late as 1738 and 1739, and seeking to assert his waning authority over his son, Charles was establishing his own image as a young, fashionable, and elegantly-dressed adult, in the portrait by Carriera that James disliked, and the strikingly mature portrayals by Hussey (Figs. 3.5 and 3.6). It was not until 1740 that James finally commissioned Domenico Dupra to paint more adult portraits of Charles.

Thus, as Corp observes, James was losing the tight control he had hitherto exercised over the public image of his son, as he had lost control between 1725 and 1727, when Clementina had followed her own artistic strategy, commissioning portraits of her sons, including two portraying Charles in Polish dress. Charles was old enough to be affected by Clementina's flight and had observed the tension between his parents after Clementina's return to the family in 1728. He had just turned 14 when she died and was greatly affected by her loss: McLynn's observations on the likely psychological impact on the young Prince are rather more convincing than his interpretation of the hair-cutting.[8]

Given that he had already sat for two portraits in Polish dress commissioned by his mother, it seems psychologically plausible in the context of his increasingly fraught relationship with his father that Charles might have asserted his attachment to Clementina, whose spectacular clashes with James he had experienced, through the commissioning of another portrait of himself in Polish dress. Might he not have invited his drawing-teacher to paint him at a time when his teenage rebelliousness was manifesting itself as a challenge to a father who, obsessed with how Charles's

[6] McLynnn 2020, 50; David Daiches. 1975. *Charles Edward Stuart. The Life and Times of Bonnie Prince Charlie*. 2nd edition: Pan, 73. Corp believes Edgar: Corp 2011, 285, n. 56.

[7] Daiches 1975, 74.

[8] McLynn 2020, 39–40.

actions might affect public perceptions of the dynasty, was nagging him constantly, while still treating him like the child he no longer was? To have himself painted in the costume of his mother's native land would have amounted to a significant and symbolic act of defiance.

Could Batoni have painted the Polish portrait? Although he only embarked on his career as a portraitist during the 1740s, he was probably engaged by James in 1738 to paint some of the six miniatures commissioned while he was still instructing the princes.[9] Charles certainly had a lasting affection for Batoni. In 1744 he wrote to Henry from Paris, urging that "Pompeo" should be engaged to copy in miniature portraits by Dupra. James, however, commissioned Veronica Telli (1717–1807) instead, although Batoni was engaged by Henry to paint a miniature copy of a new portrait of himself by Dupra.[10]

James's rejection of Batoni in 1744 suggests that he at least did not regard him as a painter of the first rank, possibly in the light of the results of the 1738 commission, or perhaps did not deem Batoni capable of realising the king's particular vision of likeness, given his closeness to his young charges. Whatever the truth, there are features of the Polish portrait that echo Batoni's first steps in the genre that he was later to make his own. Many of his early portraits depict their sitters three-quarter length, just as in the Polish portrait. Batoni drew on Roman examples, in particular, the work of Francesco Trevisani, who had worked for the Stuarts in the past, and painted the 1719 portrait of Clementina Sobieska (Fig. 3.1a):

> the background of curtains, architecture, and foliage placed immediately behind a sitter who is set close to the picture plane also derive from this source. The problem of effecting a satisfactory transition from foreground to middle ground, which Batoni was to solve so successfully in his later portraits, thus did not arise in these earliest works.[11]

The Polish portrait matches this description. Moreover, as Waterhouse has observed, in the early portraits Batoni often depicted the sitters in "fancy or masquerade dress".[12] This is particularly evident in Batoni's ear-

[9] Corp 2011, 286, n. 65.
[10] Corp 2001, 83.
[11] *Pompeo Batoni (1708–87) and his British Patrons.* 1982. London: Greater London Council, 12.
[12] Waterhouse, Ellis. 1978–80. Pompeo Batoni's Portrait of John Woodyeare. *The Minneapolis Institute of Arts Bulletin*, 64, 56–7.

liest known portrait of a British sitter, dating from 1744, which depicts Joseph Leeson, later 1st Earl of Milltown (1701–1783), who is portrayed in a peculiar fur-lined morning robe and a fur hat.[13] Even more striking is the portrait that Waterhouse was discussing, of John Woodyeare, who is depicted in a frogged uniform, with a fur-lined cloak held by a narrow chain over his shoulders, and a sash round his waist, just as in the Polish portrait (Fig. 6.1).

There is another consideration. If the Polish portrait does not reach the standard of Batoni's later work, it is worth bearing in mind that it would have been an apprentice piece. Moreover, although Batoni was a major artist who later became a consummate portrait painter in much demand, there were some who remained unconvinced by his approach, as James seems to have been in 1738. For, in the light of the doubts over

Fig. 6.1   Portrait of John Woodyeare by Pompeo Batoni (1750). Minneapolis Institute of Art Accession no. 78.24 G

[13] Clark 1985, 233–4, plate 86.

resemblance expressed by experts in Stuart portraiture with regard to the Polish portrait, it is interesting that no lesser an authority than Sir Joshua Reynolds (1723–1792) questioned Batoni's ability to catch a likeness:

> he finished his historical pictures part after part; and in his portraits completely finished one feature before he proceeded to another. The consequence was, as might be expected; the countenance was never well expressed; and, as the painters say, the whole was not well put together.[14]

If Reynolds felt this of portraits Batoni painted at the height of his powers, how much more might it have been true of would have been his earliest attempt?

None of these scenarios prove anything, of course. Batoni was in the right place at the right time, that is all. In the last analysis, the portrait, although a decent enough painting, is not of good enough quality for it to have been painted by Batoni, even at this early point in his career: his work from the 1730s, in particular his *Triumph of Venice* already exhibits a much more accomplished hand than the one that painted the Polish portrait. Furthermore, James was Batoni's employer. Batoni was surely aware of the considerable tensions between Charles and his father, and even if Charles had suggested that Batoni paint his portrait, to do so without James's approval would have risked dismissal from a post that was a significant opportunity for him.

It is possible, however, that someone else commissioned the painting, as William Hay had commissioned Blanchet to paint his 1739 portrait of Charles. The loosening of James's control over Charles's image in Rome itself is indicated by Hussey's drawings, which were not commissioned or paid for by James. Hussey seems to have had private access to the court, and his drawings were made from life. As Charles emerged into the adult world, Hay was not necessarily the only person interested in capturing his image. There was a considerable Polish community in Rome. At the time of Clementina's death, Józef Załuski (1702–1774), later bishop of Kyiv, who had served as chaplain to Stanisław Leszczyński's wife, Katarzyna Opalińska, arrived in Rome in January 1734 as Leszczyński's agent during the War of the Polish Succession. He stayed for three years, persuaded much of the substantial Polish community in Rome to support Leszczyński,

---

[14] Quoted by Clark 1985, 38.

and donated money—as did the wider Polish community—towards Clementina's funeral costs.[15]

Józef, like his brother Andrzej Stanisław (1695–1758), later bishop of Cracow, had close contacts with the Stuart court and, before her death, with Clementina. Andrzej Stanisław Załuski was a major patron of the arts and was to act as a Stuart agent in Poland-Lithuania during the long dispute over the Sobieski inheritance, and Polish artists and sculptors, such as the baroque painter Szymon Czechowicz (1689–1775), were drawn to Rome to train; Czechowicz himself stayed for two decades, between 1711 and 1731. Before the possibility of the Polish portrait being an authentic image of Charles Edward painted in the 1730s can be finally dismissed, the possibility that it was commissioned by some Polish William Hay requires investigation.

If Charles did commission the portrait, or someone else commissioned it and presented him with a copy, then it is likely that he would have kept it for himself, to hang on his walls as a permanent reminder of his mother. A considerable number of family paintings adorned the walls of the Palazzo del Re: Charles kept several in his own apartments, and when he succeeded his father in 1766, he created a family portrait gallery in the largest room in the palace.[16] Later, he took many portraits to the Palazzo Guadagni, the villa he bought in 1777 in Florence three years prior to the collapse of his 1771 marriage to Louise of Stolberg, Countess of Albany (1752–1824) in 1780.[17]

In the last years of his life, Charles moved to Rome, where he was cared for devotedly by Charlotte, his daughter by Clementina Walkinshaw, to whom he had become reconciled and whom he legitimised and created Duchess of Albany. The Palazzo Guadagni was sold and cleared. Much of the contents were sold, but personal items, including paintings, were not part of the sale and were not included in the detailed inventories that were prepared.[18] Although an inventory was drawn up of movable property sent to Rome in 1786, and his library was catalogued, once more paintings

---

[15] Loret, Maciej. 1930. *Życie polskie w Rzymie w XVIII w.* Rome: Scuola Tipografica Pio X, 22, 23.

[16] Corp 2001, 92.

[17] Louise left her husband in 1780, and the marriage was formally ended in 1784.

[18] BL Add. Ms 30745: Copia Della stima dei Miglioramente del Palazzo di Firenze Dà proprieta dà S. Altezza Lady Duchessa D'Albania', ff. 351–353v; 'Inventario della Guardaroba fatto nel miese dì Marzo 1787, ff. 354–57v.; Inventaire des Meubles du Palais a Florence avec leurs prix et estimations. f. 358; Inventario & Stima di tutti i Mobili, che si

were not included.[19] Some of his property had remained in Florence; after his death, more than 50 cases "full of valuable legacies of the late King" trundled down to Rome, where they were received by Charlotte. She immediately installed her father's library and hung "pictures of the King and other members of the Royal Family painted by famous artists" in her apartments.[20] There is no mention, however, of the Polish portrait.

Charlotte died in November 1789 of cancer of the liver; if the painting was then in her possession, it would have passed into Henry's hands.[21] The fate of the vast Stuart estate after Henry's death is murky. The principal benefactor of Henry's will was Canon Angelo Cesarini, Henry's secretary, who had looked after him faithfully in his declining years and were subsequently inherited by the wife of Count Sigismondo Malatesta. While Henry, who had been in receipt of a pension paid by George III since 1800, left some important jewels to his royal cousin, and the British government, thanks to the support and interest of the Prince Regent, the future George IV, eventually secured the Stuart Papers, much of the movable property of the last Stuarts emerged onto the market in the following years, with the Malatesta family and the English Benedictines in Rome acting as brokers. There was much interest in the Stuart legacy, and several members of the British upper classes, including Elizabeth Otway Cave, Baroness Braye, Lord Horatio Walpole, James Dennistoun of Dennistoun,

listrovano nèl Palazzo della Sig^{ra} Duchessa di Albania, ff. 359–86. The contents were valued at 9899 scudi: f. 386.

[19] BL. Add. Ms. 30475: Nota di tutto cio, che dal Palazzo di Firenze à stato mandat a Roma dopo la partenza del Sig^r Conte, e della Sig^{ra} Duchessa 24 Genno 1786, ff. 387–391; Catalogue des Livres trouvés dans une caisse au palais de S.E. Le Comte D'Albanie, ff. 393–94v. Some paintings were included in inventories of property sent to Florence when Charles bought his villa, but the Polish painting is not mentioned: RA SP/BOX/4/2/69; RA SP/MAIN/496/167; RA SP/MAIN/500/68 and RA SP MAIN/501/165.

[20] Cinquanta e più cassoni sono quelli venuti da Firenze alla Sig^{ra} Duchessa contenenti robbe e cose preziose del defonto Re da essa ereditate. Giunsero quelli venuti per mare circa la metà dello scorso Mese, e già la d^{ta} Sig^{ra} ha accommodata in una stanza spora del suo appartemento la Libreria, nella quale ha collocati i retratti dei Re e Personaggi della Casa Reali dipinti da celebri autori: *Diario per l'anno MDCCLXXXVIII di Enrico Benedetto Cardinale Duca di Yorck, Arcivesco di Corinto, Vescovo di Frascati, &c, &c, &c, ora prima stampato da un manuscritto nella biblioteca d Orazio, Conte di Orford.* 1876. London: Chiswick Press, 56–7. Tayler, Henrietta. 1950. *Prince Charlie's Daughter, being the Life and Letters of Charlotte of Albany.* London: Batchworth Press, 121.

[21] Apart from a legacy for her mother, Clementina Walkinshaw and "any necessitous relatives", Charlotte left all her property to Henry Benedict, including the garter jewel worn by Charles I at his execution: Pininski 2012, 100.

and Mr R.J. Macpherson acquired paintings, engravings, objets d'art, and other Stuart artefacts.[22]

It is unlikely, however, that the Polish portrait was among these objects. Despite the more-or-less plausible scenarios examined above, there is a point at which a historian must call a halt to the development of ever more elaborate hypotheses for which there is no evidence beyond circumstance. While it is by no means impossible that the portrait was an authentic representation of the Prince painted from life in the mid-1730s, there are too many problems that would need to be explained away if such a hypothesis were to be accepted, even apart from the fact that there is no hint of it in the contemporary sources. Nevertheless, as the detailed consideration of resemblance in Chap. 3 suggests, there is much to suggest that Helen Farquhar was justified in her view that the painting was always intended to represent Charles Edward, as the inscriptions claim. So if it was always intended to represent the Prince, as Farquhar suggests, and was not painted in the 1730s, then a different set of questions arise.

BIBLIOGRAPHY

SECONDARY SOURCES

Clark, Anthony M. 1985. *Pompeo Batoni. Complete Catalogue*. Ed. Bowron, Edgar Peters, plate 86. London: Phaidon.
Corp, Edward. 2001. *The King over the Water. Portraits of the Stuarts in Exile after 1689*. Edinburgh: Scottish National Portrait Gallery.
Corp, Edward. 2011. *The Stuarts in Italy 1719–1766. A Royal Court in Permanent Exile*. Cambridge: Cambridge University Press.
Dennistoun of Dennistoun, James. 1846. The Stuarts in Italy, *Quarterly Review*, December 1846.
McLynn, Frank. 2020. *Bonnie Prince Charlie: Charles Edward Stuart*. London: Sharpe Books.
Piniński, Peter. 2012. *Bonnie Prince Charlie, A Life*. Stroud: Amberley.

---

[22] Dennistoun of Dennistoun, James 1846. The Stuarts in Italy, *Quarterly Review*, December 1846, 149.

CHAPTER 7

The Embellishment of Tradition

Abstract The final chapter examines the question of why the portrait might have been thought to be of Charles Edward when the consensus is that it does not look like him. It considers the possibility that a painting of an anonymous Polish youth was presented as Charles Edward to cash in on the growing market in the early nineteenth century for Jacobite relics. Finally, it looks at the possibility that the portrait was painted in the nineteenth century to take advantage of the explosion of public interest in Bonnie Prince Charlie.

Keywords Jacobite material culture • Bonnie Prince Charlie • The Sobieski-Stuart brothers • Jacobitism in nineteenth-century art • Jacobitism and Romanticism

A historian is not a novelist, still less a detective novelist, even if detection is part of the challenge faced. In examining the evidence, a historian must consider the known facts and construct plausible scenarios to explain what happened, and to explain the motivation of the individuals or parties involved. Yet, although historians construct stories, as novelists construct stories, they must remain in thrall to the recorded evidence. A detective novelist constructs a scenario, peoples it with characters, and buries clues in the narrative that can be interpreted in various ways. Their significance can be skilfully disguised, in the interests of setting up the spectacular

R. I. Frost, *The Polish Portrait of Bonnie Prince Charlie*, https://doi.org/10.1007/978-3-030-99936-0_7

dénouement in the drawing room, in which a Sherlock Holmes or a Hercule Poirot reveals the truth and the novelist unveils the explanation that lay hidden in plain sight throughout.

A historian cannot control the scenario, however, and many—perhaps most—historical puzzles cannot be solved in the drawing room with the culprit exposed and Inspector Lestrade or Japp entering from the wings to make an arrest. All that can be constructed are scenarios of varying degrees of plausibility, in the hope that they suggest further avenues of research that might confirm or refute them. A historical novelist has complete freedom to choose one of the scenarios, and invent characters, situations, or psychological motivations in order to create an attractive story. A historian does not.

This book is not a historical novel, and however plausible a case can be constructed for the possibility of the Polish portrait being a genuine representation of Charles Edward Stuart painted from life in the 1730s, and however plausible the motivations that can be advanced to explain when, why, and by whom it might have been commissioned, the currently available sources do not provide anything in the way of corroboration. Thus, other scenarios need to be explored before any conclusions can be reached.

One line of enquiry is suggested by an indication that another version of the Polish portrait exists, or at least existed. In the handwritten note on its provenance in the Heinz archive, there is an intriguing piece of information that was never presented to the NPG Trustees:

> A similar picture, though smaller, is in the possession of Count Joseph Schönborn, son of Charles Count Schönborn, and Princess Jeanne Lobkowitz, and through his mother descended from the Sobieski family.[1]

No source is given for this information. It clearly derives from Gery Cullum. Josef Maria Leopold Ottomar Eugen Karl, Graf von Schönborn-Wiesentheid is an obscure figure, but a real one. He was born on 15 November 1866 in the Schönborn palace of Maleschitz (Malešice) in Moravia, the fourth son of Karl, Graf von Schönborn-Wiesentheid (1840–1908), and his wife, Johanna Prinzessin von Lobkowitz (1840–1872), and died, unmarried, in Berlin on 17 March 1914. He was interested in art and was associated with the avant-garde artist Hermann

---

[1] Heinz Archive: NPG 1929.

Bahr, who knew him in the 1890s.[2] The catalogue of the Schönborn Gallery in Pommersfelden prepared in 1857, nine years before Josef's birth, does not contain any reference to such a painting, while the three decades of war, revolution, and political turmoil into which Europe was about to be plunged on his death suggest that the fate of his estate may be difficult to track down.[3]

The Lobkowitz family had no direct descent from the Sobieskis as the note claims, but it is conceivable that a version of the Polish portrait ended up in the possession of the Schönborn or Lobkowitz families. There is an indication in the Cullum papers that Gery Cullum knew Josef Schönborn: in a letter to Cullum of 9 November 1918, Oswald Barron, after discussing his war service in the Inns of Court reserve regiment, writes: "I wonder what has happened to Schönborn. This is indeed the twilight of the German gods; even the mediatized gods will be packing for their lives".[4]

Schönborn was already dead, however, and no correspondence between him and Cullum has yet come to light. Nevertheless, if the portrait did turn out to be genuine, it is entirely possible that a version of it ended up in what became the Habsburg monarchy. After the partitions of Poland-Lithuania, Żółkiew ended up in Habsburg-ruled East Galicia. Before his move to Żółkiew, Jakub Sobieski was long resident in Silesia, having become duke of Ohlau in 1691 on his marriage, and was well-connected with the Habsburg nobility. In 1811 Charlotte, Duchess of Albany's second cousin once removed, Prince (Louis) Victor de Rohan (1766–1846), who became duc de Bouillon in 1836,[5] and Count Erwein Schönborn (1766–1840)—a noted art collector and older brother of Josef's great

---

[2] Bahr, Herman. 1996. *Tagebücher, Skizzenbücher, Notizhefte. Personnen- und Werkverzeichnis,* ii *1890–1900.* Ed. Zand, Helene, Mayerhofer, Lukas & Moser, Lottelis. Vienna: Böhlau, 212, 297, 299.

[3] *Katalog der gräflich von Schönborn'schen Bilder-Gallerie zu Pommersfelden.* 1857. Würzburg: Friedrich Ernst Thein. Neither does it appear in *Gallerie des Grafen zu Schönborn-Wiesentheid zu Pommersfelden in Gagern. 53 Blatt nach den Orignialgemälden* photographirt. (Munich, 1867).The best pieces from the collections of the Schönborn-Buchheim family were gifted to the Residenzgalerie in Salzburg in 1956: *Salzburger Residenzgalerie mit Sammlung Schörnborn-Buchheim.* 1975. Salzburg: Residenzgalerie, 15. There is no record of any painting that might match the Polish portrait.

[4] Oswald Barron to Gery Cullum, London, 9 November 1918: Papers of Gery Milner-Gibson Cullum, Suffolk Record Office, Bury St Edmunds, E2/44/69.

[5] The title had been abolished in 1795 when the sovereign duchy was annexed by revolutionary France. The duchy was revived, though not as a sovereign state, in 1814, when part of its former territory was annexed to the Grand Duchy of Luxemburg. The la Tour

grandfather—were listed as patrons and subscribers in the Prague *Privatgesellschaft patriotischer Kunstfreunde*, (the Private Society of Patriotic Friends of Art).[6] It is therefore possible that if a version of the Polish portrait was indeed painted and sent to Maria Karolina Sobieska, duchesse de Bouillon, in 1737, or if she acquired it on the death of her father in that year, it could have ended up in the hands of the Schönborn family.

What might the laconic phrase "a similar picture" mean? It could refer to a copy of the Polish portrait or possibly a companion piece representing Henry in Polish dress, although there are no precedents for such a portrait. It is more likely, however, that this "similar painting" was not a version of the Polish portrait at all, but another painting of Charles in Polish dress, probably the David portrait that was sold in Vienna in 2007, which could well have been sent by Clementina to her father during her estrangement from James (Fig. 5.2). This hypothesis is supported by the fact that although similar, Schönborn's picture was smaller, which the David painting certainly is: the Polish portrait measures 1092 × 603 cm, whereas the David measures 74 × 61 cm. The most likely explanation for Gery Cullum's connection with Josef Schönborn is that Schönborn acquired the catalogue of the 1889 Stuart exhibition, in which the Polish portrait is described but not illustrated, and wrote to Gery Cullum to say that he also owned a painting depicting Charles Edward in Polish dress.

There are several questions that need to be addressed if the Polish portrait does not date from the mid-1730s. For if the sitter does not look anything like Charles as the experts claim, and the painting either is of an unknown young Polish aristocrat or simply depicts a youth dressing up in a masquerade version of Polish costume, why would anybody think it was Charles? If it was the former, who is the sitter and how did the claim arise? Or was the painting produced in the early nineteenth century, perhaps by overpainting Charles's face on an older portrait of a Polish youth, to exploit the new wave of romantic interest in Charles? Finally, how did the portrait come into the possession of Clementina Jacobina Sobieska Schnell, née Macdonald?

d'Auvergne family had died out in the male line, and the title was conferred upon Louis Victor's older brother by the Congress of Vienna in 1815.

⁶ *Hof- und Staats-Schematismus des Österreichischer Kaiserthums.* 1811. Vienna: K.u.K. Hof- und Staatsdruckerey, 773. For Franz Erwein von Schönborn see Bott, Katherina. 1993. *Ein Deutscher Kunstsammler zu Beginn des 19. Jahrhunderts. Franz Erwein von Schönborn (1776–1840)* Alfter: Verlag und Datenbank für Geisteswissenschaften.

These possibilities, however, give rise to yet another set of problematic questions. While the story of Clementina Sobieska's arrest, escape, and marriage ensured that her part in the great Stuart romance was not forgotten, and while her Polish background—in particular, her descent from John Sobieski, the Hammer of the Turks—is usually mentioned, Charles's Polish side is otherwise almost entirely forgotten or ignored, and even when respectable historians discuss matters Polish, they sometimes display ignorance of Polish history: as careful a scholar as Nicholson writes that Clementina Sobieska was the granddaughter of "Prince" John Sobieski, "who had repulsed the Turks from Constantinople".[7] This would indeed have been a remarkable feat, but Sobieski was no prince; he was the elected king of Poland and grand duke of Lithuania, and he defeated the Ottomans at Vienna, quite a distance from the walls of Constantinople.

The problem is even more evident with regard to popular accounts: an egregious example is the entry in the 1889 Stuart exhibition catalogue describing a portrait of Clementina, which claims to have a late sighting of James's unfortunate queen in 1757, "after the breaking of her hopes and the failure of the raid on Derby, when she was 55". It states that she died on 18 January 1765 at the age of 64.[8] The march on London, which ended with the decision taken at Derby to return to Scotland, took place in December 1745, not 1757, and Clementina expired 30 years earlier, on 18 January 1735, at the age of 32. It is unclear where Sir James Drummond, who lent the portrait to the exhibition, or whoever wrote the catalogue entry for him, derived his information. Even Banquo's ghost did not hang around for three decades.

Not everyone was quite so wide of the mark, but the general lack of interest in Charles's Polish connections raises the question of why any fraudster or fantasist would have chosen to pass off a decent enough portrait of an unknown Polish teenager as Prince Charles Edward Louis Casimir, as the first inscription has it, or gone to the trouble of commissioning a reasonably competent painter to paint such an image. The burgeoning market in Jacobite relics called for hair and tartan, not sabre and sash. A reasonable-quality painting of the Prince in tartan would be much in demand, but why should any dealer who came across the Polish portrait decide that it might be a depiction of Charles or believe that it could be passed off as him if the experts are correct, and it looks nothing like him?

---

[7] Nicholson 2002, 34.
[8] *Exhibition of the Royal House of Stuart*, no. 156, 54.

It is perhaps best to approach this problem by first considering the question as to how the Polish portrait came to be in the possession of Clementina Jacobina. If the possibility that she inherited it from her father is dismissed, then she must either have commissioned it herself or have received it as a gift, or have purchased it. Clementina Jacobina was certainly a collector. According to the Reverend Edmund Farrer, who knew Gery Cullum well, "she was the source of all the Stuart relics at Hardwick".[9] This proud Jacobite, daughter of a man who had served his Prince and suffered for it, was living in Kew, a few hundred yards from the favourite palace of George III, whose son her husband had tutored before his death in 1823. She was to live for another two decades during the key period in which Jacobite nostalgia not only became fashionable, but in which the markets for Jacobite material took off, both the elite market, with the possessions of the exiled Stuarts sold off by the Malatesta family for high prices, and the secondary market of less valuable items, that encompassed the growing number of dubious relics analysed by Guthrie. It is therefore unlikely that Clementina Jacobina commissioned the portrait herself. Although she bore the name Sobieska, and therefore knew about Charles's Polish connections, it seems she was a collector, not a con-artist. The simplest explanation is that she purchased the painting from a dealer, or perhaps was given it by someone who knew of her interests.

So when and where might the portrait have been painted? It is unlikely that it was originally an eighteenth-century Polish portrait of an anonymous youth from a wealthy noble family. Apart from the question of how such a picture might have reached London, the form of Polish dress presented poses a problem. The subject wears the short form of coat known as a *bekiesza*. The *bekiesza*, however, was largely worn by poorer nobles and burghers between the sixteenth and eighteenth century, and only became more popular in wealthier *szlachta* circles in the later eighteenth and nineteenth centuries.[10] The standard garment of the Polish *szlachta* (nobility) was the *żupan*, a rich, ankle-length, long-sleeved, lined coat, usually tied with a colourful and distinctive wide Turkish-style silk belt or sash known as a *pas kontuszowy*. Over it was worn either a *kontusz*, a

[9] Farrer 1908, 161.
[10] Turnau, Irena. 1999. *Słownik ubiorów. Tkaniny, wyroby pozałkackie, skóry, broń i klejnoty oraz barwy znane w Polsce od Średniowiecza do początku XIX w.* Warsaw: Wydawnictwo Naukowe "Semper", 21.

sleeveless overgarment, frequently in a contrasting colour, or a cloak known as a *delia*.

This traditional style of dress, known widely today as Sarmatian, was a political statement. Down to the late sixteenth century, the aristocratic elite among the *szlachta* had affected western-style dress. The mass of the ordinary nobility, however, was fiercely egalitarian: all nobles were citizens, and all citizens were equal. Titles were outlawed except, under the terms of the 1569 Union of Lublin, for the title of *kniaź*—Polish *książę*— (duke) used by descendants of the ruling dynasties of Lithuania and Rus', the Gediminids and the Rurikids. Some families—such as the Radziwiłłs— who were not themselves of such elevated descent—blurred the distinction by acquiring titles from the Holy Roman Empire, which meant that the wearing of ermine in portraits became quite common, as magnate families chose to display their aristocratic status. By the mid-seventeenth century, the magnate elite had almost completely adopted Sarmatian dress, at least away from the royal court. The style had become associated with the republican Polish-Lithuanian system, with its emphasis on citizenship, elective monarchy, and an uncentralised political system, in which ultimate control lay with the noble sejmiks (dietines) at the local level, who elected envoys to the Sejm.

Western dress was widely regarded as the effete and decadent fashion of absolute monarchies. By the 1730s, however, many among the Commonwealth's magnate elite began to reject the Sarmatian style. Poland-Lithuania had gradually descended into political disorder as the result of the long series of wars it fought after 1648, which reached its nadir during the Great Northern War (1700–1721), itself in part a civil war. As calls for reform began to be made at the royal court and among the magnate elites—who could not agree on what form change should take—sophisticated aristocrats began to despise those among the unenlightened ordinary nobility who venerated the Polish-Lithuanian constitution and refused to countenance change. The Sarmatian style in consequence became associated with hidebound political conservatism. By the 1730s, magnates were beginning to have themselves portrayed once more in western dress, at least in reformist circles. To be painted in Polish dress consequently became even more of a political statement.

It is not just the dress of the sitter that raises questions. For the Sarmatian style extended to hair, including facial hair. In contrast to the long hair and goatee beards of sixteenth- and seventeenth-century western nobles, and then the wigs adopted all but universally across Europe during the reign of Louis XIV, Polish nobles grew Sarmatian moustaches and shaved their heads, often leaving a topknot. Accused by western observers of looking like Turks or Tatars, they are usually shown bareheaded, to distinguish themselves, for in the Islamic world covering the head was universal.[11] Portraits of youths are relatively rare; although they could not yet be expected to grow moustaches, when they are depicted in Polish dress, they are frequently shown bareheaded, with shaven or closely-cropped heads (Fig. 7.1) Thus, the three sons of Maksymilian Ossoliński (1640–after 1702) are depicted bareheaded in this portrait dating from the 1670s. Ossoliński himself wears an ermine-lined *kontusz* worn over his *żupan*: the Ossolińskis had acquired the title of duke from the Holy Roman Emperor in the 1630s.

Since wealthy Polish nobles often travelled to western Europe in this period, their exotic costumes attracted the attention of artists, most notably in the case of Rembrandt's *Polish Rider*, now in the Frick Gallery in New York. A few years later, another Dutch painter, Caspar Netscher (1639–1684), painted a portrait of a youth in Polish dress, traditionally claimed to be prince Sigismund Casimir Vasa (1640–1648), son of King Władysław IV (ruled 1632–1648), which bears considerable similarities to the depiction of Ossoliński's sons (Fig. 7.2). It was not until the late eighteenth century that children began to be depicted more frequently in the less cumbersome *bekiesza*.

The *bekiesza*, however, became popular outside Poland-Lithuania as the fashion for masquerades spread around Europe from about the 1720s. As the craze for dressing-up at masked balls took hold among Europe's elites, and the pleasure-gardens at Vauxhall and Ranelagh drew London's smart set, exotic styles of dress became the rage. The classic Sarmatian combination of *kontusz* and *żupan* was a little cumbersome for the masquerade, but under the influence of Hungarian more than Polish style, variants on the shorter *bekiesza* became popular, although there exists an early portrait by Alexis Simon Belle (1674–1734), of Roger Strickland (1680–1704), an exile from a strongly Jacobite family, in Polish dress, wearing a form of *żupan* and *kontusz*, and a cap that shows a distinct resemblance to that worn by the sitter in the Polish portrait. Since it was painted long before

[11] Koutny-Jones, Alexandra. 2008. Echoes of the East: Glimpses of the Orient in British and Polish-Lithuanian portraiture of the eighteenth century. In Ungar, Richard, ed. *Britain and Poland-Lithuania. Contact and Comparison from the Middle Ages to 1795.* Leiden & Boston: Brill, 414.

Fig. 7.1   Maksymilian Franciszek Ossoliński and his sons. (Anon. (1670s). Royal Castle, Warsaw ZKW/4925 Public Domain)

James III married Clementina Sobieska, however, it can have no connection with the Polish portrait.[12]

As the fashion for masquerade spread, the depiction of boys and youths in masquerade-style dress loosely based on national costumes became

---

[12] I am grateful to Rab MacGibbon for drawing my attention to this painting, which is now in Sizergh Castle, Cumbria, the home of the Strickland family: http://www.nationaltrustcollections.org.uk/object/998444

Fig. 7.2 Portrait of a Boy in Polish National Costume by Caspar Netscher (1668–1672). (Czartoryski Museum Cracow MNK XII-263 Public Domain)

increasingly fashionable, the more exotic the better.[13] A craze for Hungarian-style hussar uniforms spread in England after the War of the Austrian Succession in the 1740s, during which Britain was allied with the Habsburgs.[14] From the 1770s, the fashion affected much of Europe,

[13] Ribiero, Aileen. 1984a. *Dress in Eighteenth-Century Europe.* London: B.T. Batsford Ltd., 140–86.

[14] Ribeiro, Aileen. 1984b. *The Dress Worn at Masquerades in England 1730 to 1790, and its Relation to Fancy Dress in Portraiture.* London & New York: Garland Publishing, appendix II, 420–7.

Fig. 7.3 Portrait of a Boy in Hussar's Uniform (after 1760). (Workshop of Martin van Meytens the younger (1695–1770) ©Kunstpalast, Düsseldorf. Photo: Horst Kolberg, ARTOTHEK)

helped by Maria Theresa of Austria, who frequently dressed her young son, the future emperor Joseph II, in Hungarian dress.[15] *Portrait of a Boy in Hussar's Uniform* (Fig. 7.3), painted after 1760 by Martin van Meytens the Younger (1695–1770), who had painted James III and Clementina

---

[15] Możdżyńska-Nawotka, Małgorzata. 2020. "Dressed "as if for a Carnival": Solving the Mystery of the Origins of Children's Fashion. A New Perspective on the History and Historiography of Children's Dress, *Textile History* 51/1, 14.

Sobieska in 1725, perhaps demonstrates why. For many west Europeans, it was difficult to distinguish Hungarian from Polish dress.

As the Polish-Lithuanian Commonwealth, facing partition by its neighbours, entered its great struggle for reform in the reign of its last king, Stanisław August Poniatowski (ruled 1764–1795), who dressed in the western style, there was something of a revival of Polish-style dress among those who resisted Poniatowski's reform plans as well as the malevolent ambitions of the partitioning powers.[16] In Danzig, which was left high and dry, cut off from the Commonwealth, after the First Partition of 1772, this patriotic feeling was strong, and Johanna Schopenhauer (1766–1838), mother of the philosopher Artur Schopenhauer, fiercely opposed the looming annexation by Prussia, which finally took place at the Second Partition in 1793. She wrote about how boys were dressed in stylised forms of Polish dress to emphasise Danzig's loyalty to the kingdom of Poland.[17]

As Możdżyńska-Nawotka shows, this fashion lasted deep into the nineteenth century, and was influential across Europe, particularly at periods in which Poland was in the news, such as the first half of the 1790s, when the Second and Third Partitions shocked western Europe. The European vision of the chaotic Poland of much of the eighteenth century was being replaced outside central and eastern Europe by an image of tragic Poland mauled by its avaricious and autocratic neighbours despite the dramatic reforms of the Four-Year Sejm (1788–1792), culminating in the Constitution of 3 May 1791, which seemed to place Poland-Lithuania firmly in the progressive, Enlightenment camp, in opposition to the repressive monarchies responsible for the partitions.

The Polish Revolution and the Second and Third Partitions were for the most part favourably covered in the British press, but the period in which Samuel Taylor Coleridge, Edmund Burke, and Charles James Fox praised the Poles for their love of liberty, was relatively short-lived. Tadeusz Kościuszko, the leader of the 1794 uprising against the Russians that precipitated the Third Partition, was briefly fêted when he passed through London en route for America in 1797 despite his leading role in the American Revolutionary War, but French support for Poland during the Revolutionary and Napoleonic Wars, the creation of the Grand Duchy of

---

[16] Koutny-Jones 2008, 412.
[17] Możdżyńska-Nawotka 2020, 10–13; 18–23.

Warsaw by Napoleon, and the prominent role of Poles in the French armies down to 1815 meant that enthusiasm soon waned.

It did not die completely, however, especially in radical circles. In 1797 Coleridge's friend Henry Francis Cary (1772–1844) wrote an *Ode to General Kościuszko*, while in 1799 the Scottish poet Thomas Campbell (1777–1844) published *The Fall of Poland*, which contained the immortal line "Freedom shrieked as Kościuszko fell". Campbell compared the Polish hero to Robert the Bruce, with both presented as fighters in Freedom's cause. In 1803, the Scottish writer Jane Porter (1776–1850) published a four-volume novel about Kościuszko, inspired by her brother's meeting with him in London in 1797.[18]

Pro-Polish sentiment strengthened again after 1815, as Poland once again fell victim to the great-power politics that many had begun to question in Britain. The 1815 Congress of Vienna completed the fourth partition of Poland-Lithuania, slicing it up in a different form, while the years that followed demonstrated that the apparently liberal intentions of Emperor Alexander I in establishing the Congress Kingdom of Poland under Russian rule, with a constitution and a degree of autonomy, meant little in practice. France remained the main centre for Polish political emigres, but Polish aristocrats began visiting Britain again, many of them still under the influence of the anglophilia of the late King Stanisław August Poniatowski and his supporters.[19] Some stayed, attracted by Britain's parliamentary system that was presented as a contrast to France under the restored Bourbons, whose vain attempt to turn the sundial back to the reign of their guillotined brother, Louis XVI, collapsed in 1830. Poles in Britain sought to counter the widespread ignorance of the country's history. In 1821 a group of Polish aristocrats donated 123 books, comprising 148 volumes on Poland, some of them rare editions, to the library of the Writers of the Signet in Edinburgh. They form the core of the National Library of Scotland's collection of Polonica to this day.[20]

---

[18] Gołębiowska, Zofia. 2001. Jane Porter—angielska (sic) admiratorka Tadeusza Kościuszki. *Annales Universitatis Mariae Curie-Skladowska Lublin—Polonia* vol. LVI Sectio F, 7–23.

[19] See Butterwick, Richard. 1998. *Poland's Last King and English Culture. Stanisław August Poniatowski, 1732–1798.* Oxford: Oxford University Press.

[20] Gmerek, Katarzyna. 2021. Kolekcja polska w Bibliotece Notariuszy w Edynburgu i jej ofiarodawcy. In *Projektowanie niepodległości i dziedzictwo polszczyzny. W stulecie odzyskania niepodległości.* Ed. Ratajczak, Wiesław & Osiewicz, Marek. Poznań: Poznańskie Studia Polonistyczne, 91–109.

Interest in Poland increased considerably after the 1830 November Rising, when Britain became home temporarily—in some cases perma- nently—to a much larger number of Polish refugees. The replacement of Wellington's government by Earl Grey's Whig administration in 1830 raised the hopes of Adam Jerzy Czartoryski (1770–1861), former foreign minister to Emperor Alexander I. Czartoryski was a leader of the November Rising who became the most prominent Polish politician in exile after 1831. He had toured England and Scotland in 1790 with his mother, Izabela Czartoryska (1746–1835), and returned to Britain in 1831 to lobby for British support for the insurrection. He found that the Whig government, while more sympathetic than the Tories, was not inclined to intervene, although it did vote for an annual subsidy to support Polish emigres. Nevertheless, the *Times* took up the Polish case, and a number of pro-Polish associations were established, most significantly the Literary Association of the Friends of Poland, whose founding president was Thomas Campbell, who had rekindled his enthusiasm for the Polish cause. Pamphlets were published and a journal, *Polonia—Monthly Reports* was established to promote the Polish cause.[21]

It is against this background that perhaps the most plausible explana- tion for the painting of the Polish portrait emerges, if it does not date from the 1730s. The great revival of interest in Jacobitism in the 1820s and 1830s, in which Sir Walter Scott played such a key role, sparked Polish interest in Charles Edward and his rebellion against the Hanoverian gov- ernment, which had clear echoes of Polish struggles against the partition- ing powers, while also raising consciousness in Jacobite circles about the Stuarts' Polish connections. Clementina Jacobina was by no means the only female who bore the name of Charles's mother: the widespread prac- tice of christening children with Stuart names was a means of quietly pro- claiming Jacobite sympathies. Scots, including Jane Porter and Thomas Campbell, were prominent in advocating the Polish cause after 1830, while Lord Dudley Stuart, grandson of Lord Bute, George III's prime minister, was a leading figure in the Literary Association of the Friends of Poland.

---

[21] The best and most detailed account of changing British opinion with regard to Poland is Cybowski, Miłosz K. 2016. The Polish Questions in British Politics and Beyond, 1830–1847. Doctoral thesis, History, University of Southampton, 2016. https://eprints. soton.ac.uk/403552/. The reaction to the November Rising is covered extensively in chap- ter four, 91–130.

A growing number of wealthy Poles were also attracted by the Stuart story. This was in part due to the Catholicism of the Stuarts: the magnificent tombs of Clementina and her husband and sons in St Peters in Rome, where many Poles made pilgrimages, drew attention to the Stuart cause, while there was still a strong awareness of the large number of Scottish migrants who had flocked to Poland-Lithuania in the sixteenth and seventeenth centuries. Izabela Czartoryska, Adam Jerzy's mother, did not tour Scotland on a mere whim. A prominent writer and intellectual, who had run a renowned and progressive Enlightenment salon in the last years of the Polish-Lithuanian Commonwealth, Izabela, like all the Czartoryskis, was very conscious of the family's Scottish roots. They were descended from Catherine Gordon (1635–1691), daughter of George Gordon, 2nd Marquis of Huntly, a leading Catholic nobleman from northeast Scotland, who had been executed in 1649 during the Wars of the Three Kingdoms. Catherine was born in exile in Paris; with her twin brother Henry, she was brought up at the Polish court in the entourage of Queen Louise Marie Gonzaga (1611–1667). In 1659 she married the baroque poet and politician Jan Andrzej Morsztyn (1621–1693); Stanisław August Poniatowski, Poland's last king, was her great grandson through his mother, Konstancja Czartoryska.

Izabela was fascinated by Scotland. She had read James Macpherson's *Ossian*, probably in French translation, and describes an evening in a Perthshire inn after her coach broke down, in which she encouraged the locals to sing Ossianic melodies; she was convinced by their authenticity and rejected the attacks on Macpherson, led by Samuel Johnson, who claimed that his Ossianic works were forgeries. Her son, Adam Jerzy, was also impressed by Scotland: his later poem *The Polish Bard*, contained literary allusions to Ossian, Robert Burns, and John Gray's poem *The Welsh Bard*.[22] Adam Jerzy's nephew, Adam Konstanty Czartoryski (1804–1880) took after Izabela, his grandmother. He became an enthusiastic Scotophile, studying at Edinburgh University, and was one of the donors to the Signet Library. He joined the Caledonian Horticultural Society, the Speculative Society, and the Celtic Society, of which Walter Scott was the animating

---

[22] Gmerek, Katarzyna. 2013. Scotland in the eyes of two Polish lady travellers. In *Scotland in Europe/Europe in Scotland Links—Dialogues—Analogies*, ed. Szymańska Izabela & Korzeniowska, Aniela. Warsaw: Wydawnictwo Naukowe "Semper", 1–4. The original manuscript of the journal, written mostly in French, is in the Czartoryski Library in Cracow, which was founded by Izabela.

spirit. The Scottish papers reported that Adam Konstanty attended Celtic Society meetings dressed in tartan.[23]

Thus, although consciousness of Poland remained relatively low among the broader British public, it was much higher in Jacobite circles. Clementina Jacobina's very name proclaimed the Sobieski connection, so she was certainly aware of it. It is therefore plausible that she would be interested, as a collector of Stuart relics, in pieces that proclaimed and embodied their Polish connections. It seems that Gery Cullum assumed— or was told by his stepmother, Ann Cullum—that Clementina Jacobina acquired the painting from her father, and that he had been given it by Charles Edward or his father, an assumption given a degree of verisimilitude by the story that she was James III's—or Charles's—goddaughter. While it seems reasonable to suppose that Clementina Jacobina told Ann Cullum the latter story, there is no evidence that she said anything about the provenance of the portrait, or how she acquired it.

It is most likely that she bought it to add to her collection of Stuart relics, just as it is likely that she bought the locket now in the Moyse's Hall Museum (Fig. 2.3). Although her acquisition of the David des Granges miniature of Charles I, which the NPG gratefully accepted, suggests that she was capable of acquiring genuinely valuable pieces, despite her enthusiasm for the Stuarts, she seems not to have had the most discerning of eyes: some of the Stuart paintings from Hardwick House, judging by the photographs exhibited in the Spanton-Jarman collection, are not of the highest quality, while several of them were misidentified.[24] An elderly lady of fiercely Jacobite sentiment spending money in the growing market for Jacobite relics and images of the Stuarts would certainly have attracted the attention of dealers; it is entirely possible that one of them who became aware of any interest in the Polish connections of the Stuarts, might have

[23] Gmerek 2021, 97.

[24] On the advice of Edward Corp, the following identifications were changed in the Spanton-Jarman online catalogue of Hardwick portraits: K505-2987, previously catalogued as unknown man is a copy of one of the Belle portraits of James III painted in France between 1708 and 1712, or more likely an engraving of one of those portraits; K505-2988, previously catalogued as unknown lady, is a copy of a 1719 David portrait of Clementina Sobieska; K505-3094, previously catalogued as a young lady is not a lady at all, but a copy of an engraving based on David's 1723 portrait of Charles Edward as a young boy, K505-3781, catalogued as an unknown gentleman is probably James II; K505-3787, previously catalogued as James Francis Edward Stuart (i.e., James III and VIII) is actually a copy of one of the two 1740 Dupra portraits of Charles.

arranged to provide her with a portrait that embodied them so consummately.

As Guthrie has shown, there was much dubious practice in the secondary market for Jacobite material in Britain in the 1820s and 1830s. It may be simply a coincidence, but nevertheless it is striking that the 1820s and 1830s, the period in which Clementina Jacobina was building up her collection, was also the period in which those magnificent con-artists and rogues, the Sobieski-Stuarts reached the giddy heights of their fame. The grandsons of one admiral in the Royal Navy and the nephews of another, John (c. 1795–1872) and Charles Allen (c. 1799–1880) adopted their ultimate identities in stages. Their first grand entrance came at the Edinburgh pageant mounted for George IV in 1822, when they appeared in the elaborate version of Highland dress that was to become their trademark, outshining many of the clan chiefs who paraded Edinburgh's streets. John, who was already calling himself Hay Allen—his brother had become Charles Stuart Allen—marked the occasion by publishing 42 annotated romantic poems of Highland lore. The Allen was soon discarded, as the brothers claimed descent from Charles Hay, the last earl of Erroll. He had died a bachelor in 1717, but that minor inconvenience did not trouble the enterprising brothers. The mere claim was enough for John to have sported the emblem of the High Constable of Scotland—the hereditary office of the Hays—during the king's visit.[25]

By the late 1820s, the brothers had charmed their way through those sections of London and Scottish society that were beguiled by misty Jacobite romanticism. Walter Scott, who had done so much to start that particular bandwagon trundling, was not fooled. He had noticed the badge of the High Constable of Scotland during the 1822 pageant and pointed out that the Hay Allens, as they then styled themselves, had no right to wear it. When they began discreetly to spread word of their possession of several mysterious manuscripts, which, they hinted—they did not really claim—had been presented to their father by Charles Edward himself. One, in particular, dated 1571 but supposedly much older, was to form the basis for their two sensational books on the origins of tartan and Highland dress, the *Vestiarium Scoticum* (1842) and *The Costumes of the Clans* (1845), published long after Scott was safely dead, for when the brothers had begun to publicise their possession of the mysterious

---

[25] Trevor-Roper, Hugh. 2008. *The Invention of Scotland. Myth and History*, 218–9. New Haven, MA: Yale University Press. Nicholson 2002, 110.

manuscript, Scott challenged them to produce it for proper investigation. When they failed to do so, citing a litany of excuses, Scott dismissed them as frauds.[26] Scott's flinty Whig head always kept his Tory heart under control.

The story of the Sobieski-Stuarts is well known. After Scott's death in 1832, they gradually revealed the sensational back story at which they had merely hinted at first—that their father Thomas Allen—whom they began to style Duke of Albany—was the son of Charles Edward and his wife, Louise Stolberg. He had, so they claimed, been smuggled out of Italy as a baby and given into the care of their grandfather, Admiral John Carter Allen. By the mid-1830s, they were being fêted in aristocratic castles across Scotland. Their greatest admirer, Thomas Alexander Fraser, 12th Lord Lovat (1802–1854) set them up in Eilean Aigas, their Scottish Neuschwanstein, on an island in the river Beauly, where they held court until their downfall following a devastating demolition in the 1847 *Quarterly Review* of the *Vestiarium Scoticum* and *Tales of the Century*, a thinly disguised *roman-à-clef* which told the tale of their alleged descent in highly coloured prose.[27] Its anonymous author—now believed to be George Skene (1807–1875), Professor of Law at Glasgow University—relentlessly probed their increasingly bizarre fantasies and exposed the extent of their fraudulent scholarship.[28] Thereafter, with their reputation punctured, and deprived of the support of Lord Lovat, who died in 1854, the brothers could no longer find patrons ready to indulge them and had to give up their fantastic establishment, ending their days in poverty in London, where they continued to conduct their idiosyncratic version of research in the Reading Room of the British Museum.

There have been attempts recently to rehabilitate the Sobieski-Stuarts, at least in part, based on their research into Highland culture. They had taught themselves Gaelic, and carried out detailed research into Gaelic sources, while interviewing Gaelic speakers to explore the rich oral culture

---

[26] Trevor-Roper 2008, 221–2. Stuart, John Sobieski. 1842. *Vestiarium Scoticum: from the Manuscript formerly in the Library of the Scots College at Douai.* Edinburgh: William Tait. Stuart, John Sobieski Stolberg & Stolberg Stuart, Charles Edward. 1845. *The Costumes of the Clans.* Edinburgh: J. Menzies.

[27] Stuart, John Sobieski & Stuart, Charles Edward. 1847. *Tales of the Century, or Sketches of the Romance of History between the Years 1746 and 1846.* Edinburgh: Marshall.

[28] *Quarterly Review*, vol. 81 (June–September, 1847), 57–85.

of the Highlands.[29] Yet neither Skene nor Hugh Trevor-Roper—who regarded the brothers with a degree of benevolent affection—denied that the Sobieski-Stuarts carried out some genuine scholarship; the problem is that the results are so entangled with their fantasies that it is impossible to take their works seriously. Hugh Cheape, who mounts an effective challenge to those who have used the Sobieski-Stuarts to dismiss the notions that tartan is of ancient origin in Scotland, and that individual clans had their own patterns, nevertheless has to admit that their versions of clan tartan were "undoubtedly fake".[30]

The Allen brothers were undoubtedly fakes, but they were also scholars, and they knew of Charles Edward's Polish connection. They became the Hay brothers in the 1820s; it was not until the 1830s that they became the Sobieski-Stuarts, sometimes adding "Stolberg" to buttress their claim that their grandmother was Louise Stolberg, which, if true, would have made their father the legitimate Stuart heir. The addition of "Sobieski" came at precisely the time that Poland, thanks to the November Rising, had forced itself into British public consciousness.

In the Scotland of the 1830s, in the context of the romantic resurgence of interest in the Jacobite past, Poland's plight had a particular resonance. The *Caledonian Mercury* for 18 February 1837 printed an extensive report of a magnificent "Polish Fancy Ball" held in the Assembly Rooms, George Street, Edinburgh, to raise money for Polish refugees who were not in receipt of one of the small grants the British governments had allocated for their relief. It was a glittering occasion with an impressive turnout from the great and the good of Scottish society, including Edinburgh's Lord Provost, Sir James Forrest, first Baronet of Comiston; Lord Abercromby; Lord Gifford; Lord Elibank; and Lord Charles Kerr. A large body of stewards received the company in the vestibule. They wore the "distinguishing badge of a white and red rose, bound with ribbon of the same colour, being the national colours of Poland". Roses were not of any particular significance as a symbol of Polishness; the white rose, however, was one of the most powerful and evocative Jacobite symbols. There was a large military contingent from the Scottish regiments in dress uniform;

---

[29] Holder, Julie. 2019. The Sobieski-Stuarts and the Garderobe of Scotland. *History Scotland*, 19/5 (Sept–Oct 2019).

[30] Cheape, Hugh. 2016. Gheibhte breacain charnaid ("scarlet tartans would be got..."): the re-invention of tradition. In Brown, Ian, ed. *From Tartan to Tartanry. Scottish Culture, History and* Myth. Edinburgh: Edinburgh University Press, 15, 22.

others came in masquerade dress: the Misses Thomson and Charlton were reported as wearing "elegant Polish Ladies' costume". It was reported that their dresses "from the richness of their material, and correctness, excited universal attention, and were amongst the most admired objects in the room". Ranald George MacDonald (1788–1873), 20th Chief of Clanranald and grandson of the Young Clanranald who had welcomed Charles to Scotland alongside Donald MacDonald of Kinlochmoidart, was there. Despite overseeing the sale of almost all of his estates since 1813—a process that was to be completed the year after the Polish ball— he turned out "in the complete Highland garb, girt with the sword presented to him by King George IV, being that worn by Charles Stuart in his expedition in 1745".[31]

The Sobieski-Stuarts were not listed among the guests, but against such a background, their revival of the Sobieski name seems a calculated move. Both the brothers were skilful draughtsmen, painters, woodcarvers, and furniture makers, who decorated Eilean Aigas with a range of paintings and objects designed to buttress their claims and exalt their supposed ancestry.[32] By the testimony of Charles-Victoire Prévot, vicomte d'Arlincourt (1788–1856), the wildly popular French romantic novelist, who visited Eilean Aigas in 1843, the main hall contained a portrait of Charles Edward Stuart, and a painting of Culloden by John Sobieski-Stuart, whose execution, according to d'Arlincourt, "was as fine as its conception"; opposite to it was one that was "no less remarkable" of Napoleon at Waterloo, reflecting the unlikely claim of the brothers that they had fought for Napoleon at the 1813 battle of Leipzig.[33]

There is no evidence that the Sobieski-Stuarts painted the Polish portrait of Charles Edward, and such examples of their artistic technique that are known suggest that they were not sufficiently skilful to produce a painting of this quality. Nevertheless, they were active in artistic circles and in the market for Stuart memorabilia. The addition of Sobieski to their names had helped revive consciousness of Charles Edward's Polish forebears and to bring together romantic Jacobite sentiment and the pro-Polish feeling among the Scottish elite that was on such splendid display in the Assembly Rooms in February 1837.

[31] Anon. 1837. The Polish Fancy Ball. *The Caledonian Mercury* 18 February 1837.
[32] Trevor-Roper 2008, 220.
[33] Beveridge, Hugh. 1909. *The Sobiesk- Stuarts and their Claim to be descended from Prince Charlie*. Inverness: Robert Carruthers, 95–6.

It is entirely possible that, in such an atmosphere, some Jacobite sympathiser might have conceived the idea of cashing in by commissioning a portrait of Charles Edward in Polish dress that took account of his portraits, and in particular, to the Lemoyne bust, which Biggar Blaikie and Charles himself saw as such a good likeness. By the 1830s, there were plenty of artists producing paintings of greatly varying quality of Charles Edward and his escapades, and there were enough representations of his face in circulation for a reasonably talented artist to create an image that bore some resemblance to him. At least one contemporary artist, Thomas Duncan (1807–1845), is said to have modelled Charles's features on the Lemoyne bust in his painting of Charles entering Edinburgh in 1745 after the battle of Prestonpans, which was first exhibited in 1840.[34]

In many respects, this explanation seems the most satisfactory. Someone, perhaps inspired directly or indirectly by the Sobieski-Stuarts, decided to produce an image of Charles Edward in Polish dress, and a dealer in Jacobite relics sold it to the proud daughter of a veteran of the '45, beguiled by her father's tales who had honoured his memory by collecting Stuart artefacts. Since the Sobieski-Stuarts were active in Jacobite circles in London in the 1820s before their move to Eilean Aigas, it is entirely possible that they knew, or had heard of Clementina Jacobina, and passed on her name. Perhaps it was at her instigation that the second inscription was added, with its error concerning Charles's place of death. Or perhaps it was added by a dealer, concerned that the first inscription was not informative enough.

Nevertheless, while this may indeed be the most plausible hypothesis of all, there are two nagging questions that will not go away. Why would an artist who wished to paint a fancy portrait of Charles in the 1820s or 1830s, and used the Lemoyne bust and other portraits as models, portray his subject as an adolescent? The Lemoyne bust was made of the adult, not the teenage Charles. Why take ten years off him? If Charles's Polishness was felt to be associated more with his childhood, why not simply copy one of the well-known David, Liotard, or Blanchet portraits of Charles as a child, and dress it up in a *bekiesza*? And why not fake a more helpful inscription than "Prince Charles Edward Louis Casimir", which clearly required what amounts to an elaborate painted footnote to explain it? Of course, if the faker had come across a genuine eighteenth-century portrait of a youth in Polish dress—whether of a real Polish adolescent or of a

---

[34] Nicholson 2002, 117.

teenager in masquerade—then it would have been appropriate to paint a youthful face. Nevertheless, it does seem rather too much effort to expend to dupe an elderly lady.

It is time to end the questions and the speculation. The author of this book is a Scottish historian, but he is not a historian of Scotland, still less a historian of Jacobitism or an art historian. He has no definitive answer to a problem that has intrigued him since he first came across this remarkable image. Seeking that answer has taken him on the strangest of journeys from the aching beauty of Kinlochmoidart to the faded gentility of Kew Green and the decaying Sobieski palace of Żółkiew, now Zhovkva in western Ukraine, via the Suffolk Record Office in Bury St Edmunds and the Central Archive of Old Acts in Warsaw. The best answer he can give is that the Polish portrait was probably, as Helen Farquhar suggested, always intended to represent Prince Charles Edward Louis Casimir Stuart.

Whether it was painted in the 1730s or the 1830s remains an open question. The NPG conservation records reveal that the picture is painted on a plain weave canvas that has been glue-paste lined onto a similar but finer canvas support, but the removal of the original tacking edge makes dating of the canvas more difficult. The painting is not of a standard size, which can be useful in identifying date ranges, but less so in this case, since it is not clear how much of the original canvas was cut away in the relining process. It is possible that an x-ray might reveal whether the face has been overpainted, and while investigation of the pigments used might help date the picture, there is no guarantee that it would enable a definitive judgement to be reached as to whether it was painted in the early eighteenth or the early nineteenth century. Given the considerable demands on the NPG's limited budget, it is understandably reluctant to devote resources to further technical investigation of a portrait of a subject whose identity, say the experts, is doubtful, and which therefore remains officially classified as an "unknown man".

So, alas, there is no Sherlock Holmes or Hercule Poirot on hand to step forward and provide a neat solution to this intriguing puzzle. The purpose of the book has been twofold: apart from considering the painting itself, which is interesting in its own right, it has sought to emphasise that the history of the Stuarts during their long exile in Italy cannot be understood without considering the Polish dimension of Jacobitism. Quite apart from the vexed question of the battle for the Sobieski inheritance after 1740, there is much more that still needs to be researched on that front, not least concerning the court of Clementina's relation, Stanisław Leszczyński, duke of Lorraine and father-in-law of Louis XV, whose court hosted Charles himself on several occasions, and was a hotbed of freemasonry and a magnet for Jacobite emigres. Investigation of those links might give rise to yet another hypothesis concerning the portrait's origins.

Whenever it was painted, however, the story of the Polish portrait and its acquisition by an unusually interesting collector of Stuart memorabilia provides a good example of the powerful attraction of Jacobitism in the years after Walter Scott published his *Waverley*. Nicholson sees the 1820s as a period which was marked less by "the manufacture of fresh commemorative objects than the manufacture of a bogus past for existing objects", as part of a continuing process of "recycling the past to suit modern sensibilities".[35] It seems that the Polish portrait, whether or not it was authentic, was used in the early nineteenth century not so much to invent tradition as to embellish it. As such, it is certainly interesting, and perhaps deserves to be taken out of the NPG store and exhibited again as a significant and idiosyncratic element in the nineteenth-century reimagining of the Jacobite past.

BIBLIOGRAPHY

HEINZ ARCHIVE, NATIONAL PORTRAIT GALLERY, LONDON

NPG 1929.

SECONDARY SOURCES

Farrer, Rev. Edmund. *Portraits in Suffolk Houses.* 1908. London: Bernard Quartich.

Gmerek, Katarzyna. 2021. Kolekcja polska w Bibliotece Notariuszy w Edynburgu i jej ofiarodawcy. In *Projektowanie niepodległości i dziedzictwo polszczyzny. W stulecie odzyskania niepodległości.* Ed. Ratajczak, Wiesław & Osiewicz, Marek, 91–109. Poznań: Poznańskie Studia Polonistyczne.

Koutny-Jones, Alexandra. 2008. Echoes of the East: Glimpses of the Orient in British and Polish-Lithuanian portraiture of the eighteenth century. In Ungar, Richard, ed. *Britain and Poland-Lithuania. Contact and Comparison from the Middle Ages to 1795,* 401–19. Leiden & Boston: Brill.

---

[35] Nicholson 2002, 109.

Możdżyńska-Nawotka, Małgorzata. 2020. 'Dressed "as if for a Carnival": Solving the Mystery of the Origins of Children's Fashion. A New Perspective on the History and Historiography of Children's Dress', *Textile History* 51/1 (2020), 5–28.

Nicholson, Robin. 2002. *Bonnie Prince Charlie and the Making of a Myth. A Study in Portraiture 1720–1892*. Cranbury, NJ, & London: Associated University Presses.

Trevor-Roper, Hugh. 2008. *The Invention of Scotland. Myth and History*. New Haven, MA: Yale University Press.

Bibliography

Primary Sources

Archives

Heinz Archive, National Portrait Gallery, London

NPG 1924.
NPG 1929.
Wortley, Clara Stuart. 1948. Data from the Stuart Papers at Windsor dealing with the Portraits of the Royal Stuarts. Prepared by the Hon. Clara Stuart Wortley and edited, after her death, by Henrietta Tayler. 1948.

The Royal Archives, Windsor

The Stuart Papers.
Box 4/2/69; 106/12; 281/168; 281/177; 321/119; 177/31; 194/33; 199/166; 327/50; 356/27; 366/176a; 432/147; 496/167; 500/68; 501/165.

© The Author(s), under exclusive license to Springer Nature Switzerland AG 2022
R. I. Frost, *The Polish Portrait of Bonnie Prince Charlie*, https://doi.org/10.1007/978-3-030-99936-0

SUFFOLK RECORD OFFICE, BURY ST EDMUNDS

E2/26/1. Copy of the Will of George Gery Milner-Gibson-Cullum Esq. Dated 19th September 1921.
E2/37.2. Genealogical papers of the Cullum family and other papers.
E2/44/69. Papers of Gery Milner-Gibson Cullum.

BRITISH LIBRARY

Add. Ms 30745.

ARCHIWUM GŁÓWNE AKT DAWNYCH, WARSAW

Archiwum Radziwiłłów.
Dz. III: Correspondence with members of ruling houses.
47 Correspondence of Clementina Sobieska, 1728–1734.
51 Papers of James Stuart. 1739–1740.
249 Correspondence of Charles Edward Stuart.
276 Correspondence of James Stuart.
277 Correspondence of James Stuart, 1737–1762.

PRINTED PRIMARY SOURCES

Anon. 1937. The Polish Fancy Ball. *The Caledonian Mercury* 18 February 1837.
A review of the two late rebellions, historical, political and moral. Part the first. Containing, I. A succinct account of the rebellion in the year 1715. II. The rebellion in 1745, to the end of the first consultation at Derby, as taken from the notes of General MacDonald, aid de camp to the Young Chevalier, 1745. 1747. London: R. Baldwin jun.
A Selection of Scottish Forfeited Estates Papers 1715–1745. 1909. Ed. Miller, Alexander H. Edinburgh: Publications of the Scottish History Society, vol. 67.
Bahr, Herman. 1996. *Tagebücher, Skizzenbücher, Notizheft. Personnen- und Werkverzeichnis,* ii *1890–1900.* Ed. Zand, Helene, Mayerhofer, Lukas & Moser, Lottelis. Vienna: Böhlau.
Exhibition of Stuart and Cromwellian Relics and Articles of Interest connected with the Stuart Period at the Guildhall Cambridge, May 15–20, 1911. 1911. Cambridge: John Clay & Sons at the University Press.
Diario per l'anno MDCCLXXXVIII di Enrico Benedetto Cardinale Duca di Yorck, Arcivesco di Corinto, Vescovo di Frascati, &c, &c, &c, ora prima stampato da un manuscritto nella biblioteca d Orazio, Conte di Orford. 1876, 56–7. London: Chiswick Press.

Exhibition of the Royal House of Stuart. The New Gallery, Regent Street. 1889. London & Bungay: Richard Clay & Sons Limited.

Historical and Genealogical Account of the Clan or Family of Macdonald from Somerlett, King of the Isles, Lord of Argyll and Kintyre, to the present period, more particularly as relating to the senior branch of that family, viz. the Clan Ranald. 1819. Edinburgh: D. Stevenson & Co.

Hof- und Staats-Schematismus des Österreichischer Kaiserthums. 1811. Vienna: K.u.K. Hof- und Staatsdruckerey.

Journall and Memoirs of P…C… Expedition into Scotland &c. 1745–6. By a Highland Officer in his army. In Lockhart, George. 1817. *The Lockhart Papers,* 2 vols. London: Anderson.

Katalog der gräflich von Schönborn'schen Bilder-Gallerie zu Pommersfelden. 1857. Würzburg: Friedrich Ernst Thein.

King, William. 1818. *Political and Literary Anecdotes of his Own Times.* London: John Murray.

Memorials of John Murray of Broughton, sometime secretary to Prince Charles Edward, 1740–1747. 1898. Ed. Bell, Robert Fitzroy. Edinburgh: Publications of the Scottish History Society, vol. 27.

Miller, Lady Anne. 1776. *Letters from Italy in the Years 1770 and 1771.* 2 vols. London: Edward & Charles Dilly.

Milner-Gibson-Cullum, G. Gery, ed. 1928. *Genealogical Notes relating to the Family of Cullum from the Records of the Heralds' College, the Hardwick House Collections, Wills, Registers etc.* London: Michael Hughes & Clarke.

Mounsey, George Gill. 1846. *Authentic Account of the Occupation of Carlisle in the 1745 by Prince Charles Edward Stuart.* London & Carlisle: Longman and Co.; James Steel.

Origins of the 'Forty-Five and Other Papers Relating to that Rising. 1916. Ed. Blaikie, Walter Biggar. Edinburgh: Publications of the Scottish History Society, vol. 2.

Papendick, Charlotte. 2015. The Memoirs of Charlotte Papendick. In *Memoirs of the Court of George III.* Vol. i. Ed. Kassler, Michael. London: Routledge.

Recollections of Marshal Macdonald, Duke of Tarentum. 1893. Ed. Rousset, Camille; trans. Stephen Louis Simeon. New York: Richard Bentley & Sons.

Reports of Cases decided in the High Court of Chancery by the Right Honourable Sir Lancelot Shadwell, Vice-Chancellor of England, volume VII, *Containing Cases in 1834, 1835 & 1836, with a Few in 1837.* 1937. Ed. Simons, Nicholas. London: J. & W.T. Clarke.

Salzburger Residenzgalerie mit Sammlung Schörnborn-Buchheim. 1975. Salzburg: Residenzgalerie.

Sobiesciana z archiwum hr. Przezdzieckich w Warszawie. 1883. ed. Leniek, Jan. Cracow: Czas.

Stuart, John Sobieski. 1842. *Vestiarium Scoticum: from the Manuscript formerly in the Library of the Scots College at Douai*. Edinburgh: William Tait.

Stuart, John Sobieski Stolberg & Stuart, Charles Edward Stolberg. 1845. *The Costumes of the Clans*. Edinburgh: J. Menzies.

Stuart, John Sobieski & Stuart, Charles Edward. 1847. *Tales of the Century, or Sketches of the Romance of History between the Years 1746 and 1846*. Edinburgh: Marshall.

The Lyon in Mourning. A collection of speeches, letters, journals relative to the affairs of Prince Charles Edward Stuart. 1895–1896. Ed. Paton, Henry. 3 vols, i, 289–90. Edinburgh: Publications of the Scottish History Society, vols 20–22.

The Trial of Æneas Macdonald, Banker to the Pretender at Paris. 1748. London: Price.

Westminster Journal or New Weekly Miscellany, 1 November 1747.

ONLINE

Archives Parlementaires de 1787 à 1860. Première Série: de 1789 à 1799, vi: 1789— États généraux. Cahiers des sénéchaussées et bailliages. 1879. Ed. Mavidal M.J. & Laurent, E. tome vi. Paris: Librairie administrative de Paul Dupont. Online version: Tome 6 : 1789 – États généraux. Cahiers des sénéchaussées et baillages [Toul - Vitry-le-François].

Kilkenny Archaeological Society, in Irish Archives Resource: http://www.iar.ie/ Archive.shtml?IE%20KAS%20Q010.

http://les.guillotines.free.fr/guillo-m.htm.

http://www.geneanet.org/archives/releves/search_etat_civil.php?search=FALC OZ+DE+LA+BLACHE+D%27HARNONCOURT&id_table=5294&lang=fr.

Spanton   Jarman   Project   https://www.burypastandpresent.org.uk/ gallery-viewer/.

SECONDARY SOURCES

Anon. 1847. Review of the *Vestiarium Scoticum* & *Tales of the Century*. *Quarterly Review*, vol. 81 (June–September, 1847), 57–85.

Anon. 1938. A Link with Prince Charlie, *The Times*, 27 September 1938.

Anon. 1954. Oil Paintings Auctioned. Sale of Bury Collection, *Bury Free Press*, 25 June 1954.

Beresford Chancellor, E. 1894. *The History and Antiquities of Richmond, Kew, Petersham, Ham, &c*. Richmond: Hiscoke.

Blaikie, Walter Biggar. 1897. *The Itinerary of Prince Charles Edward from his landing in Scotland July 1745 to his departure in September 1746*. Publications of the Scottish History Society vol. 23. Edinburgh: Edinburgh University Press.

Bott, Katherina. 1993. *Ein Deutscher Kunstsammler zu Beginn des 19. Jahrhunderts. Franz Erwein von Schönborn (1776–1840)* Alfter: Verlag und Datenbank für Geisteswissenschaften.

Browne, James. 1838. *A History of the Highlands and of the Highland Clans*, four vols. Edinburgh & London: Fullarton & co.

Burke's Landed Gentry of Great Britain. The Kingdom in Scotland. 2001. 19th edition, ed. Beauclerk Dewar, Peter. Chicago & London: Burke's Peerage and Gentry LLC.

Butterwick, Richard. 1998. *Poland's Last King and English Culture. Stanisław August Poniatowski, 1732–1798.* Oxford: Oxford University Press.

Cheape, Hugh. 2016. Gheibhte breacain charnaid ("scarlet tartans would be got…"): the re-invention of tradition. In Brown, Ian, ed. *From Tartan to Tartanry. Scottish Culture, History and* Myth. Edinburgh: Edinburgh University Press.

Clark, Anthony M. 1985. *Pompeo Batoni. Complete Catalogue.* Ed. Bowron, Edgar Peters, plate 86. London: Phaidon.

Clarke de Dromantin, Patrick. 2005. *Les Réfugiés Jacobites dans la France du XVIIIᵉ siècle. L'exode de toute une noblesse pour cause de religion.* Bordeaux: Presses universitaires de Bordeaux.

Corp, Edward. 2001. *The King over the Water. Portraits of the Stuarts in Exile after 1689.* Edinburgh: Scottish National Portrait Gallery.

Corp, Edward. 2011. *The Stuarts in Italy 1719–1766. A Royal Court in Permanent Exile.* Cambridge: Cambridge University Press.

Cybowski, Miłosz K. 2016. The Polish Questions in British Politics and Beyond, 1830–1847. Doctoral thesis, History, University of Southampton, 2016. https://eprints.soton.ac.uk/403552/.

Davis, Natalie Zemon. 1984. *The Return of Martin Guerre.* Cambridge, Mass. Harvard University Press.

Dennistoun of Dennistoun, James. 1846. The Stuarts in Italy, *Quarterly Review*, December 1846.

Farquhar, Helen. 1923–1924. Some portrait medals struck between 1745 and 1752 for Prince Charles Edward. *British Numismatic Journal* 17, 171–225.

Farrer, Rev. Edmund. Between 1921 & 1928. *Hardwick Manor House, Bury St Edmunds and its Evolution.* Place of publication unknown: Publisher unknown.

Farrer, Rev. Edmund. *Portraits in Suffolk Houses.* 1908. London: Bernard Quartich.

Forsyth, David. 2017. *Bonnie Prince Charlie and the Jacobites.* Edinburgh, National Museums Scotland.

Frost, Robert. 1993. *After the Deluge. Poland-Lithuania and the Second Northern War 1655–1660.* Cambridge, Cambridge University Press.

Fulford, Roger. 1973. *Royal Dukes. The Father and Uncles of Queen Victoria.* Revised edition. London: Harper Collins.

Gmerek, Katarzyna. 2021. Kolekcja polska w Bibliotece Notariuszy w Edynburgu i jej ofiarodawcy. In *Projektowanie niepodległości i dziedzictwo polszczyzny. W stulecie odzyskania niepodległości*. Ed. Ratajczak, Wiesław & Osiewicz, Marek, 91–109. Poznań: Poznańskie Studia Polonistyczne.

Gmerek, Katarzyna. 2013. Scotland in the eyes of two Polish lady travellers. In *Scotland in Europe/Europe in Scotland Links—Dialogues—Analogies*, ed. Szymańska Izabela & Korzeniowska, Aniela. Warsaw: Wydawnictwo Naukowe "Semper".

Gołębiowska, Zofia. 2001. Jane Porter—angielska (sic) admiratorka Tadeusza Kościuszki. *Annales Universitatis Mariae Curie-Składowska Lublin—Polonia* vol. LVI Sectio F, 7–23.

Greenblatt, Stephen. 1980. *Renaissance Self-Fashioning: From More to Shakespeare*. Chicago: University of Chicago Press.

Gregg, Edward. 2003. The financial vicissitudes of James III in Rome. In Corp, Edward & Fowle, Francis, eds. *The Stuart Court in Rome. The Legacy of Exile*. Aldershot: Ashgate.

Grosvenor, Bendor. 2008. The Restoration of King Henry IX. Identifying Henry Stuart, Cardinal York. *The British Art Journal* IX/1 (2008), 28–32.

Guthrie, Neil. 2013. *The Material Culture of the Jacobites*. Cambridge: Cambridge University Press.

Holder, Julie. 2019. The Sobieski-Stuarts and the Garderobe of Scotland. *History Scotland*, 19/5 (Sept–Oct 2019).

Jagodzinski, Sabine. 2013. *Die Türkenkreige im Spiegel der polnisch-litauischen Adelskultur. Kommemoration und Represäntation bei den Żółkiewski, Sobieski und Radziwiłł*. Studia Jagiellonica Lipsiensia Bd 13. Ostfildern: Jan Thorbecke Verlag.

Koutny-Jones, Alexandra. 2008. Echoes of the East: Glimpses of the Orient in British and Polish-Lithuanian portraiture of the eighteenth century. In Ungar, Richard, ed. *Britain and Poland-Lithuania. Contact and Comparison from the Middle Ages to 1795*, 401–19. Leiden & Boston: Brill.

Lenman, Bruce. 1984. *The Jacobite Risings in Britain 1689–1746*. London: Eyre Methuen.

Libiszowska, Zofia. 1980. Ród Sobieskich w Europie po śmierci Jana III, *Sobótka* 35/2.

Loret, Maciej. 1930. *Życie polskie w Rzymie w XVIII w*. Rome: Scuola Tipografica Pio X.

Macdonald, Angus & Macdonald, Archibald. 1896–1904. *The Clan Donald*, 3 vols. Inverness: Northern Counties.

Macdonald, Rev. Charles. 1989 (reprint of 1889 edition). *Moidart; or Among the Clanranalds*. Edinburgh: James Thin.

Mackenzie, Alexander. 1881. *The Macdonalds of Clanranald*. Inverness: A. & W. Mackenzie.

McDonnell, Frances. 1999. *Highland Jacobites 1745*. Baltimore MD: Clearfield.

McLynn, Frank. 2020. *Bonnie Prince Charlie: Charles Edward Stuart*. London: Sharpe Books.

Monod, Paul. 1989. *Jacobitism and the English People 1688–1788*. Cambridge: Cambridge University Press.

Możdżyńska-Nawotka, Małgorzata. 2020. 'Dressed "as if for a Carnival": Solving the Mystery of the Origins of Children's Fashion. A New Perspective on the History and Historiography of Children's Dress', *Textile History* 51/1 (2020), 5–28.

Nicholas, Donald. 1973. *The Portraits of Bonnie Prince Charlie*. Maidstone: Clout & Baker.

Nicholson, Robin. 2002. *Bonnie Prince Charlie and the Making of a Myth. A Study in Portraiture 1720–1892*. Cranbury, NJ, & London: Associated University Presses.

Nicholson, Robin. 1998. The tartan portraits of Charles Edward Stuart. *British Journal for Eighteenth-Century Studies*. 21, 145–60.

No Quarter Given. The Muster Roll of Prince Charles Edward Stuart's Army, 1745–46. 2001. Ed. Livingstone, Alastair, Aikman, Christian & Stuart Hart, Betty. Glasgow: Neil Wilson.

Vitelleschi, Amy, Marchesa. 1903. *A Court in Exile. Charles Edward Stuart and the Romance of the Countess d'Albanie* 2 vols. London: Hutchison & Co.

Norie, William Drummond. 1903–1904. *The Life and Adventures of Prince Charles Edward Stuart* 4 vols. London: Caxton.

Pappe, Bernd & Schmieglitz-Otten, Juliane. 2008. *Miniaturen des Rokoko aus der Sammlung Tansey*. Munich: Hirmer Verlag.

Piniński, Peter. 2012. *Bonnie Prince Charlie, A Life*. Stroud: Amberley.

Piper, A. Cecil. 1943. Clementina Jacobina Sobieski. *Notes and Queries*, 185/7. 25 September 1943.

Platania, Gaetano. 1980. Angielskie małżeństwo Marii Klementyny. *Sobótka*, 35/2.

Pointon, Marcia. 1993. *Hanging the Head. Portraiture and Social Formation in Eighteenth-Century England*. New Haven & London: Yale University Press.

Redstone, Lilian J. 1911. Hardwick House, Bury St Edmunds. *Proceedings of the Suffolk Institute of Archaeology*, xiv, part 2, 267–74.

Ribiero, Aileen. 1984. *Dress in Eighteenth-Century Europe*. London: B.T. Batsford Ltd.

Ribeiro, Aileen. 1984. *The Dress Worn at Masquerades in England 1730 to 1790, and its Relation to Fancy Dress in Portraiture*. London & New York: Garland Publishing.

Sankey, Margaret & Szechi, Daniel. 2001. Elite culture and the decline of Scottish Jacobitism, 1716–1745. *Past & Present*, 173, 90–128.

Schmidt-Liebich, Jochen. 2005. *Lexikon Der Kunstlerinnen 1700–1900. Deutschland, Österreich, Schweiz*, 184–5. Berlin: De Gruyter Saur.

Shield, Alice. 1908. *Henry Stuart, Cardinal of York*. London: Longmans, Green & Co.

Skrzypietz, Aleksandra. 2015. *Jakub Sobieski*. Poznań: Wydawnictwo Poznańskie.

Skrzypietz, Aleksandra. 2011. *Królewscy synowie—Jakub, Aleksander i Konstanty Sobiescy*. Katowice: Wydanwnictwo Uniwersytetu Śląskiego.

Skrzypietz, Aleksandra. 2003. Maria Karolina de Bouillon i jej kontakty z Radziwiłłami. In Stępnik, Krzysztof, ed. *Radziwiłłowie. Obrazy literackie. Biografie. Świadectwa historyczne*. Lublin: Wydawnictwo Uniwersytetu Marii Curie-Skłodowskiej.

Smith, Annette. 1982. *Jacobite Estates*. Edinburgh: J. Donald.

Tayler, Henrietta. 1950. *Prince Charlie's Daughter, being the Life and Letters of Charlotte of Albany*. London: Batchworth Press.

The Prisoners of the '45. 3 vols. 1928. Ed. Gordon Seton, Bruce & Gordon Arnot, Jean. Edinburgh: Publications of the Scottish History Society. Series 3, vols 13–15.

Trevor-Roper, Hugh. 2008. *The Invention of Scotland. Myth and History*. New Haven, MA: Yale University Press.

Turnau, Irena. 1999. *Słownik ubiorów. Tkaniny, wyroby pozatkackie, skóry, broń i klejnoty oraz barwy znane w Polsce od Średniowiecza do początku XIX w*. Warsaw: Wydawnictwo Naukowe "Semper".

Vaughan, Herbert M. 1906. *The Last of the Royal Stuarts. Henry Stuart, Cardinal Duke of York*. London: Methuen.

Wallon, H. 1880–1882. *Histoire du Tribunal Révolutionnaire de Paris. Avec le Journal de ses Actes*, 6 vols. Paris: Libraire Hachette et Cie.

Waterhouse, Ellis. 1978–80. Pompeo Batoni's Portrait of John Woodyeare. *The Minneapolis Institute of Arts Bulletin* 64, 54–61.

Wyld, Helen & Dalglish, John. 2017. "A slim sword in his hand in battle". Weapons fit for a Prince. In Forsyth, David, ed. *Bonnie Prince Charlie and the Jacobites*, 79–93. Edinburgh: National Museums Scotland.

Index[1]

[1] Note: Page numbers followed by 'n' refer to notes.

© The Author(s), under exclusive license to Springer Nature Switzerland AG 2022
R. I. Frost, *The Polish Portrait of Bonnie Prince Charlie*,
https://doi.org/10.1007/978-3-030-99936-0

Printed in Great Britain
by Amazon

46283646R00086